Building and Running A Cloud Native Product

Rahul Kandhari
Prafull Verma
Kalyan Kumar

December 2019

ISBN-978-0-578-62723-6

FOREWORD

The software industry is a fast-paced and highly competitive world. I already learned the basics from browser-based frontends to distributed backends starting from the age of 15. Not so long ago, I studied computer science and at that time, the term cloud computing was still not well known. And now, cloud is everywhere. Not only the largest enterprises in the world are cloud native platform businesses, but also many small and mid-sized companies are becoming software businesses with significant parts running in the cloud.

Software developers become some of the most powerful people in the world! Why? Because we are changing so many people's experiences each and every day with technology. Of course, developers have to keep pace with the latest cloud technologies, and businesses also need to understand this. It is important for business leaders to recognize that they should not do cloud just for the sake of technology or cost reasons. The cloud transformation should rather improve their existing business processes and reinvent them over and over again. Only in this way, can enterprises prevent themselves from being disrupted by cloud native competitors.

The good news is, it's never too late to start your cloud native journey. Therefore, this book is a great starting point. The authors are practitioners who started their IT journey in the client-server area and transitioned step-by-step to become cloud native, while always keeping the business in mind. So, regardless whether you have an IT or business background, the book will cover both perspectives and will help you to get the most out of the cloud.

From a CTO perspective, this book helps to tackle two major challenges that customers face along their cloud journey. On the one hand, there is a mindset challenge. The way cloud native technologies are used, and cloud native apps are built is quite different from former times. On the other hand, it's a change in the technology itself. New programming languages, frameworks, architectures and IT infrastructures have been established. In addition, people working in this new world need to be able to efficiently leverage them. If you know these challenges, I recommend that you read this book.

For me, this book is a guide to the cloud native world for beginners as well as for experienced professionals. It provides the whole picture of cloud native development and the software product lifecycle, covering product management and increased business agility as well as more development-centric topics such as microservices, the 12-factor app methodology or continuous deployment. Finally, you will learn how to build, deploy, and maintain a cloud native product for your company.

Enjoy reading and stay curious!

Juergen Mueller

By Juergen Mueller, CTO and Executive Board Member, SAP SE

TABLE OF CONTENTS

1 PREFACE ... 1
2 LEGACY ERA TO MODERN WORLD ... 4
2.1 EVOLUTION OF SOFTWARE ARCHITECTURE ... 6
2.2 PRE-INTERNET ERA ... 7
2.2.1 The emergence of Client-server Architecture ... 7
2.2.2 Building Client-Server Application - Considerations ... 9
2.2.3 Running Client-Server App ... 12
2.3 INTERNET ERA ... 14
2.4 CLOUD ERA ... 17
2.4.1 Application Architecture on Cloud ... 19
2.4.2 IaaS - What is it suitable for? ... 24
2.4.3 PaaS - What value it delivers ... 26
2.4.4 SaaS- The modern business model ... 27
3 EMERGING ENTERPRISE STRATEGY: PRODUCT & PLATFORM ... 29
3.1 PRODUCT MANAGEMENT ... 32
3.1.1 Product management ... 34
3.1.2 Product Management Lifecycle ... 35
3.1.3 Product-Centric mindset ... 37
3.2 APPLICATION MANAGEMENT ... 42
3.3 BUILDING AN ENTERPRISE APPLICATION WITH A PRODUCT MINDSET ... 43
3.4 MVP- THE FOUNDATION OF BUILDING THE PRODUCT ... 48

3.5 AGILITY 51
3.5.1 Insanity in agility expectations 52
3.5.2 MVB is the foundation of Agility 55
3.6 EFFORT AND DURATION ESTIMATES 56
4 CLOUD NATIVE 60
4.1 DEVOPS 61
4.1.1 The idea to product- Process perspective 65
4.2 CI/CD 68
4.3 CONTAINER 74
4.4 MICROSERVICE 81
4.4.1 IP Network constraints for Microservices 84
4.4.2 Augmentation over IP networks for Microservices 88
4.4.3 Service Mesh: The right augmentation for CN world 94
4.5 DEGREE OF CLOUD NATIVITY 98
4.6 MIGRATION TO CLOUD 101
4.7 CLOUD NATIVE DOES NOT NECESSARILY MEAN ROBUST 103
4.7.1 Best Practice for Robust Application 105
4.7.2 The general guidance for robustness 106
4.7.3 Robustness of code vs. robustness of operations 107
4.7.4 Robust programming in the DevOps model 109
4.7.5 Jugaad culture and robustness 109
4.8 ECONOMICS OF CN APPLICATIONS 115
5 CORNERSTONE OF CLOUD NATIVITY 117
5.1 MICROSERVICE ARCHITECTURE 117
5.1.1 Advantages 119
5.1.2 Pre-requisites 119
5.1.3 Challenges and Remediation 121
5.2 12FACTOR APP METHODOLOGY 125
5.3 APPLYING 12FACTOR APP METHODOLOGY 126
5.4 OTHER IMPORTANT FACTORS 136
5.5 DEPENDENCY HELL 149
6 BUILD THE PRODUCT 153
6.1 DEVELOPMENT ENVIRONMENT ON PAAS 157
6.2 NEED FOR A LAB 161
6.3 SPRINT MANAGEMENT 162

6.3.1 Sprint management lifecycle 164
6.4 ROLE OF QUALITY ASSURANCE 166
6.5 DISTRACTIONS 168
6.6 COMPOSING/ASSEMBLING A PRODUCT 169
7 RUNNING PRODUCT IN SAAS MODEL 174
7.1 THE BUSINESS SUBSTANCE IS THE CODEBASE 174
7.2 DEPLOYMENT TECHNOLOGY AND ARCHITECTURE 178
7.3 FUNCTIONAL TEAMS IN OPERATING MODEL 183
8 PRODUCT MAINTENANCE 190
9 ANNEXURE: SPECIALIZED CLOUD - IPAAS 193
9.1 DATA INTEGRATION PATTERNS107 196
9.2 APPLICATION INTEGRATION PATTERNS 199
10 ABOUT THE AUTHORS 202

1 PREFACE

All three of us(authors) have been working in a service provider company. Our journey in the direction of building a product started more than fifteen years ago when we got into repeated projects of IT Service Management tool implementation. For all practical purposes, it is an ERP of IT or a packaged application implementation in each project. It goes through the complete application development lifecycle that includes coding for the customization of several business rules that are not part of the standard packaged application. In several cases, we landed up doing ample customizations that eclipsed the functionalities of the original product, but it was still an implementation, not the product build. Since we were in the business of implementing and supporting such packaged applications, we also developed tools and utilities for deployment and support. These tools and utilities were software products but meant for our use. The frequency of repetitive implementation of best practices was overwhelming, so we decided to build a standardized customization layer as an experiment that can be bolted on the top of the COTS application to create an advanced service management application. This layer itself got established as a product. Just like any other product, it has a roadmap, multiple releases, and numerous customer deployments, and a product support organization. The success of this experiment-

commercializing an add-on layer on top of the COTS application within a service company - was the first point in our journey of building a product. We were shielded from the complexity of the platform and used the application itself as the platform. We formed an island of a software division within the boundary of a service provider company, and our company was as good as our captive customer. Well, this was the mindset and the foundation of our experience in building a product. We were also exposed to the real customers - the customers of the service provider company who will use our products, and in doing so, we faced the competition as well. However, we remained in the service management domain and kept on enhancing our product to meet the emerging needs of the customers in that domain. We were, however, restricted or constrained by the limitations of the underlying platform, which was a commercial ITSM application being used by us as a platform.

By 2015, we had gathered enough expertise in the service management domain, and we realized that our underlying platform for building advanced service management application was not good enough. We foresaw the cloud computing and XaaS models dominating the IT landscape in an enterprise, and that led us to publish the principles and guidelines on managing the services in the XaaS model in the form of a book- Foundation of XaaS in the year 2016. All the then vendors of service management products were still sticking to the old concept, and so we decided to venture into building a fresh new product altogether as the next generation IT Service Management and ITSM application that will revolve around the XaaS catalog. It was our formal entry into the club of a commercial software product organization (of course, under the umbrella of a service provider parent company). Here we carried the mindset of being an independent organization with a charter of being a real software product company.

After three years, we had developed products that are Cloud Native with microservices architecture and API-first design, built on cloud foundry PaaS, have new customers, and success story. We completely adopted the product and platform approach. Because of the parent company, we had excellent exposure to how enterprise application development work, and we realized that many principles of product and platform approach could be adopted by enterprises as well and not just the product organizations. Through this book, we are happy to share our knowledge and experience with all IT generalists and communities, with the hope that it will be useful for them in enhancing their learning.

2 LEGACY ERA TO MODERN WORLD

Legacy in our context is the era where the concept of software engineering started with the growing need for control systems. NASA's Apollo program was instrumental in starting and nurturing software engineering as a discipline though it was not exactly the intent. What they did was to lay the foundation of software engineering. That was the period of so-called legacy systems, and after that complexity of the software architecture grew with time.

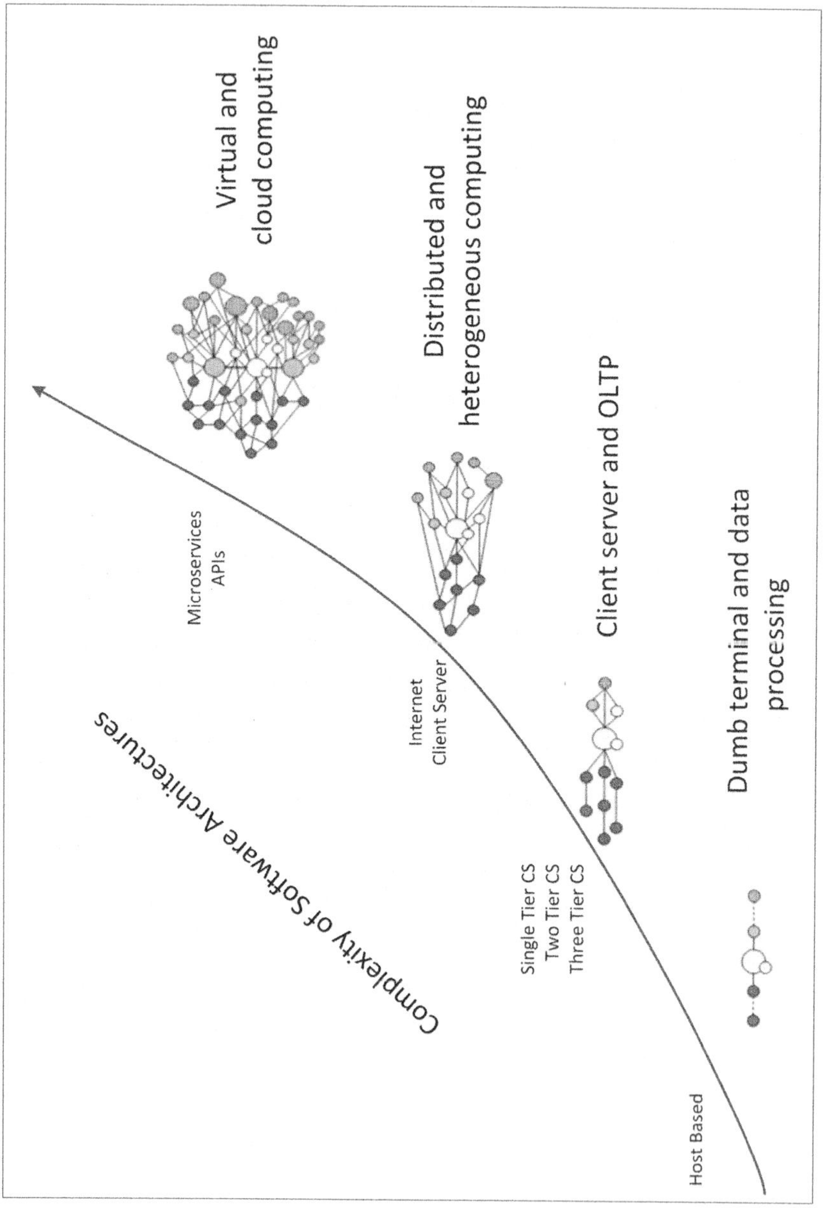

Figure 1: Growing Complexity of Software Architecture

Figure 1 is a reasonably good representation of the four different eras of computing from terminal and mainframe to the virtual and cloud computing mapped with the software architectures.

2.1 Evolution of software architecture

Although software design, development, deployment, and run of software applications are as old as mainframe itself. NASA most effectively used software engineering as a formal discipline in its Apollo program. According to The Wall Street Journal, the Apollo 11 computer that controlled the man on the moon mission, required about 145,000 lines of code in all, compared with about 62 million lines of code needed today to operate Facebook and more than two billion lines of code for Google. During this era, enterprises had the option to choose a vendor (IBM, Digital, CDC, Wang, Fujitsu, Honeywell, etc.), and a complete stack with vendor's architecture would come along with it. The buyer had no say in the architecture. The success contributor was the worthiness of the vendor in assuring the integrated/full-stack solution.

The real momentum in software design, development, deployment, and run started from the late '80s when the client-server architecture emerged after the proliferation of personal computers. It was the era when open architectures for software applications started to emerge. In the late '80s and early '90s, enterprises got the option to choose the architecture, and correctness of the selected architecture also became one of the success criteria.

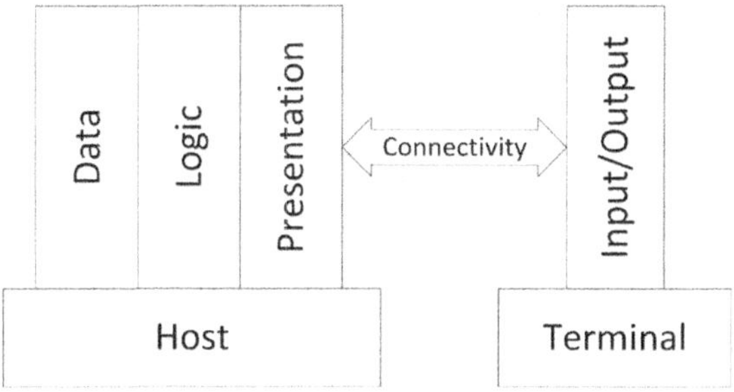

Figure 2: Software Architecture before Client Server Era

Later in the Internet era, multiple frameworks emerged; and based on those frameworks, it was possible to "assemble your architecture". Assembling your architecture is the default approach, and with the emergence of Cloud Native architecture, it has got established in every enterprise.

Today, software is everywhere and resides at the core of every business. Software architectures are mostly microservices and API-based. The API economy is emerging rapidly. API Economy is the usage of APIs to expose the company's digital product and services. It is directly related to monetary benefits, although the benefits may not be accounted for directly in most business models. API Economy is a matter of API monetization that is "driving revenue using APIs". One of the subsets of revenue-driving is charging for the use of your APIs. The business will build APIs to monetize an asset, and a third party will pay you for accessing the API either per call, or in groups of calls. API monetization is just a subset of the complete spectrum of API economy.

2.2 Pre-Internet era

The root of today's software application engineering goes as deep as the pre-internet era when the client-server architecture was the de facto architecture, and even today, while that architecture is sitting at the foundation, it is worthwhile to understand the foundation.

2.2.1 The emergence of Client-server Architecture

Client-server is a software application architecture which involves splitting the components (data, logic and presentation and yes in those days, these were the only component categories. We shall see later that in Cloud Native world the number is even more.) of an application across different processes and communicating via middleware connected on the network. So, what was the application software before that? It was then called a host-based single-tier application, and we suppose that only that the people born before 1970 would have built it. A client-server software application, at that time, was also classified as a first-generation and second-generation client-server. In first-generation, it could be two-tiered or three-tiered depending upon whether you place the three components in two different layers or three different layers. The second generation was more often called network-centric client-server software application or distributed client-server application, where these three components used to be distributed across multiple nodes in a network.

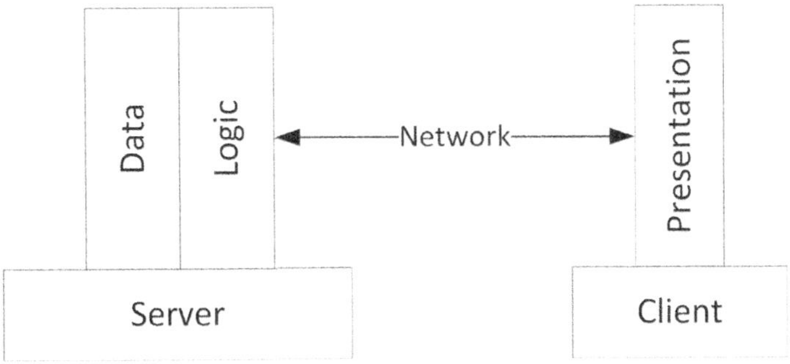

Figure 3: Two-Tier Client-Server Architecture

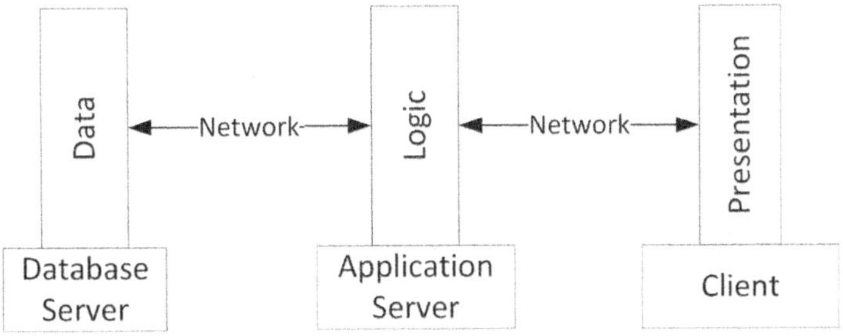

Figure 4: Three-Tier Client-Server architecture

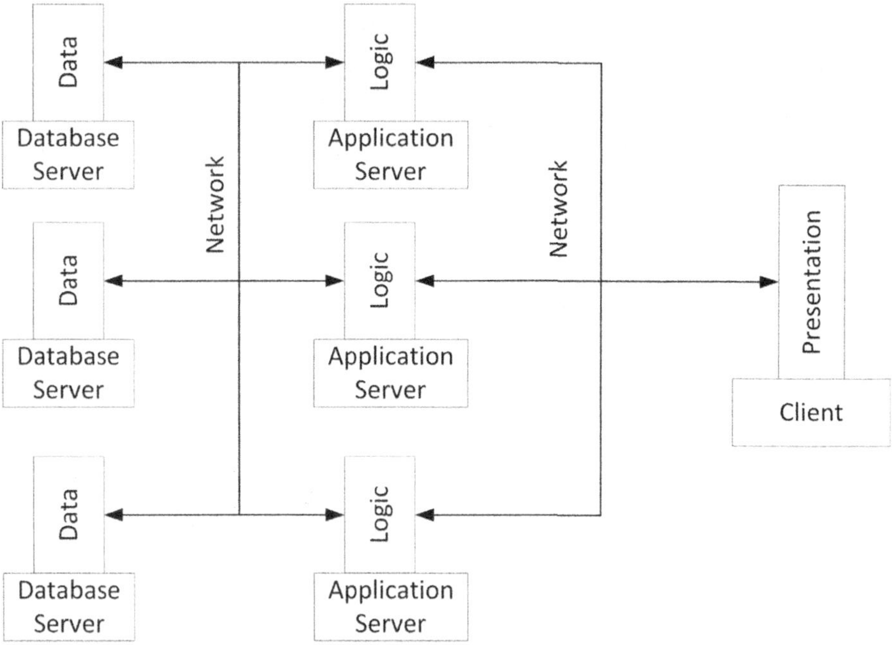

Figure 5: Network-Centric Client-Server Architecture

2.2.2 Building Client-Server Application - Considerations

Here are the essential considerations for building a client-server application. The intent is not to detail out for explanation but to brief the historical perspective and to make the audience understand that the fundamentals are still at work.

Architecture

- Concurrent connections – How many concurrent connections can be supported?
- Load sharing - Multiple servers to handle multiple simultaneous procedure calls, distributed remotely, or placed locally.
- Server Availability – Building redundancy by having multiple

servers in a cluster to provide automatic failover in case of single node failures or building redundancy by having geographically distributed servers.

- Network - Protocols to establish connectivity between a server and a client machine as well between two servers.
- Tiers or number of layers - Presentation, data, and logic separated or residing on the same or more servers.

Application Design

- Type of Client - The client could be thick or thin. Typically, the client application consists of only UI and forms in client-server applications. However, the application design could also require business logic to be handled in the client software partially or wholly. The client used to be termed as thick or thin based on whether there is a business logic handled in the client or not. The client is always responsible for rendering the user interface.
- Business Logic distributed - A client could make serial or parallel requests to multiple servers for requesting the same service.
- Security and Access Controls - Authentication used to be password-based with password matching embedded in the application logic. The user passwords used to be stored as part of the application data itself with varying levels of encryption and encryption logic used to be built within the application logic — the authorization to access various records used to be based on privileges assigned to the user. The privileges could be on multiple parameters - role or group or individual.
- Jobs - Automations required - batch v/s real-time, status monitoring
- Server affinity - Connection strings and parameters embedded in installable v/s being configurable.

Database Design

- Schema - Design of tables, and constraints
- Jobs - Backup, and maintenance of transaction logs and archives
- Capacity Requirements - Initial, auto growing by percentage or value
- Distributed or centralized - Distributed database systems for load balancing or failovers
- Replication strategy for distributed databases
- Partitioning approach - Horizontal or vertical for distributed databases
- Type of database - Analytical or OLTP
- Transaction Volumes - Storage and memory requirements

Deployment

- Resources required
    - Estimating requirements of resources for the server considering peak volume requirements. A server program could be handling requests from multiple clients as well as making requests to various other programs on the same or different servers at the same time.
    - Client machine resources required for connecting to one or more servers - A client could be connected to multiple servers due to various applications running on the same client. The software could be running locally or through virtual network connectivity.
    - Network bandwidth required for the client to server connectivity.
- OS compatibility - Compatibility of application installable with client OS.
- Compatibility of application versions - Compatibility of a client version with various server versions and vice versa.
- Distribution of installable - Server supported versions across multiple clients.

- Disaster Recovery - Getting the application to keep running from an alternative server in case of a server failure.

The purpose was to deliver a robust solution to the business, and that is still the same, slightly more critical because of technology coming to the very core of the business. However, several considerations have radically changed, as we shall see in the Cloud Native world in later sections. One of the examples is dealing with an essential exercise on deciding about the tiering factor. General guidance would say to use two tiers when we have homogeneous servers, read-only applications, and simple transactions involving a single server. Three layers were recommended when there are multiple and heterogeneous servers, complex transaction/business logic, asymmetric input streams, and a large number of clients.

Modern applications are much more complex, and significant architectural consideration is the number of layers in which the computing can be divided. Simple applications required simple segregations - data, logic, and presentation. However, complex applications need breaking the business logic layer into multiple applications, or even data layer being broken into partitions - all hosted separately on one or more than one server. The grouping of the specific functionalities guides the division an application has to fulfill as separate applications for the reason of having independent performance, scalability, restoration, upgrade, or even technology requirements.

2.2.3 Running Client-Server App

Critical considerations for running or operating the solution include:

Server

- Application Monitoring

    - Ensure every version upgrade should not lead to an outage on existing clients.
    - Ensure the resources allocated for the application use are sufficient.
    - Ensure that the application can handle transaction loads the architecture is designed for.

- Performance Monitoring
    - Ensure every version upgrade should not lead to any performance impact on existing clients.
    - Ensure that the application can handle transaction loads the architecture is designed for.

- Job Monitoring
    - Ensure that every job completed as per the frequency and schedule it needs to run at in order to take any corrective action if required.

Database

- Schema - Database remains normalized and consistent with every version release.
- Jobs - Ensure that every job completed as per the frequency and schedule it needs to run at in order to take any corrective action if required.
- Monitoring of capacity utilization - Allocated capacity should always be sufficient to meet the requirements.

Client

It is important to note that in the earlier era of client-server computing, every server application required a client application running at the user desktop/laptop to access it. The browser became a universal client at a later stage when the Web application server became an integral part of the client-server application in the Internet era. Therefore, client-side maintenance was also required in addition to the server-side support. Typical maintenance activities include:

- Availability of client software installable – A new version of the server application may need a new client software version.
- Maintenance of compatibility between versions - Client versions should be supported by a server version and vice versa.
- Resource requirement checks - to ensure that with each version upgrade on the application server, the client resources remain adequate.

User Support

- Continuous support to the users on application issues and queries.
- Continuous support for installing the correct version of the client.
- Continuous support notifying the release of a new application version.
- Continuous support notifying changes in client version requirements with a new application version.

2.3 Internet Era

Business going online became an absolute necessity, and this brought with it two dominating application architectures – one around J2EE and another around Microsoft .Net.

Java 2 Platform—Enterprise Edition (or simply J2EE) is a middleware technology first introduced by Sun Microsystems at the beginning of the Dotcom era, and Sun Microsystems was among the hottest companies that came with the slogan "we are a dot in dotcom". J2EE is a standard middleware architecture, proposed by Sun Microsystems for developing and deploying multitier, distributed, e-enabled, enterprise-scale business applications. Applications written for J2EE standards enjoy certain inherent benefits such as portability, security, scalability, load-balancing, and reusability. Specifically, for an e-commerce solution, it was a packaged architecture that was the de facto choice in that era before Microsoft came with a competitive .NET framework. The .NET framework first came in 2002, is a framework from Microsoft that provides an environment to develop, install, and execute software on Windows-based operating systems. Since Windows was the dominating operation system during that time, Microsoft got some advantage for its adoption, though the e-commerce projects were an unchallenged ground for J2EE.

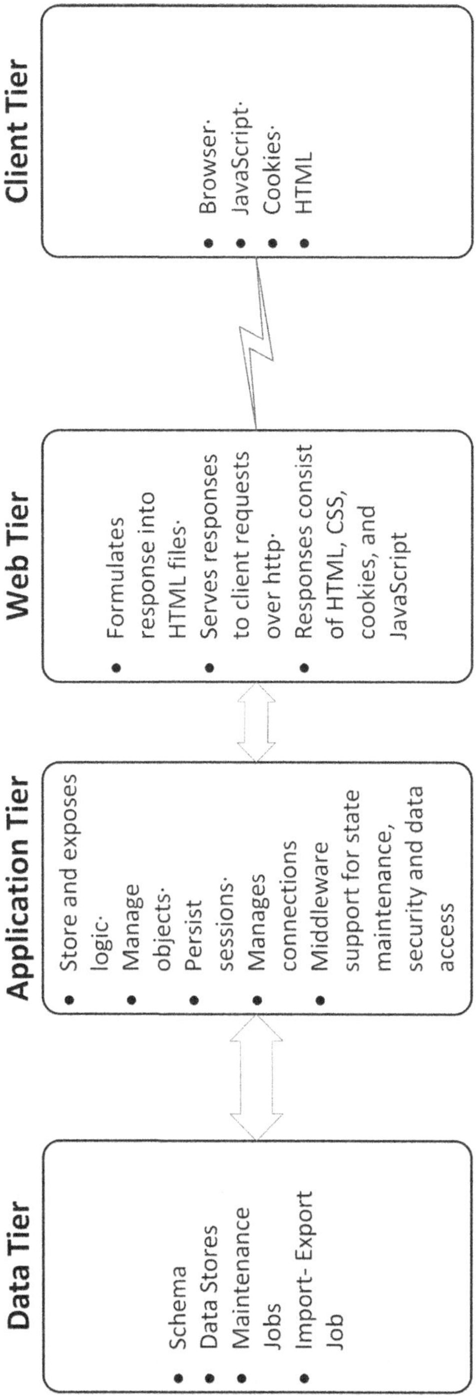

Figure 6: De facto Application Architecture in the Internet Era

Distributed computing got even more distributed with middleware and the Internet. Two-tier and three-tier client-server applications were no more modern. Middleware products were developed to manage the complexity of the application build and run, but middleware itself became a complex and significant part in the application landscape, and enterprise IT needed to have the expertise and dedicated team for middleware only.

2.4 Cloud Era

Cloud era brought in the concept of on-demand provisioning and scaling of IT compute resources. It brought in a radical change in how the enterprises are consuming IT services. Cloud era brought in changed ways to exploit virtualization and computing resources and that too, with economies of scale. The elastic computing model supporting on-demand provisioning and scalability has turned out to be the watershed of consumption patterns of how IT services were consumed before this era.

Cloud era also offers pre-built solutions consisting of on-demand services and platforms, removing the need for organizations to maintain specialized staff for the maintenance. It has let developers focus on what they like doing the most - develop the code, and loosening up the tangles of requiring the platforms, environments, and services provisioned and maintained for the system to run. The adoption of the cloud is increasing by the day, and most of the enterprises have now adopted the cloud-first approach, i.e., all new applications or reviews of existing applications will first consider cloud-based services before anything else.

Cloud era brought the following benefits to the enterprises:

- Agility - On-demand self-service-based provisioning and

auto-scaling of computing resources and other cloud-based services like databases, monitoring, auto-scaling, testing, etc. has increased the rapidity of new solutions leading to business agility.
- Accessibility - Standard access methodologies for various services across various devices have improved the usage of the IT services.
- Utility-based - Services are metered just like public utilities requiring enterprises to pay only for what they consume.
- Global footprints - Ability to use data centers around the globe ensure that enterprises can offer services to their customers from data centers closer to the end-users.

By the time the cloud era came into prominence, enterprises already had lots of applications running in their then existing IT infrastructure. As the cloud-based services started to gain popularity, the enterprises began to adopt various approaches to migrate their applications to the cloud. The new apps were being considered to be anyways available on the cloud. The adoption started with the cloud extending their existing IT infrastructure and specific tasks being dedicated to run on the cloud. It also could be used to handle overflows or back office or scheduled IT job activities, thus guaranteeing a certain level of performance for such services or activities.

The cloud era is the era in which we live today, and as we write this book, the world continues to see upward trends in its popularity.

Cloud presents three deployment models:
1. Public - The resources are owned and managed by a third party and are provided over the internet. You can manage and access the services through a browser.
2. Private - The resources are meant for exclusive use by one

enterprise. The cloud can either be hosted by the enterprise data center or by a third party. Services are available only on a private network.

3. Hybrid - It's a mix of the enterprise data center, private cloud, and public cloud deployments. The data and applications can be hosted and flow across public and private clouds.

The considerations for these deployments are:

1. Criticality - Mission criticality, security sensitiveness
2. Type of workload - Data volumes, latency requirements
3. Cost to setup
4. Elasticity required
5. Security threats
6. Multi-tenancy - single machine sharing by multiple customers

2.4.1 Application Architecture on Cloud

Applications with client-server architecture and J2EE architecture have been migrated to the cloud, but software architecture for the application natively built on cloud is depicted in figure 7.

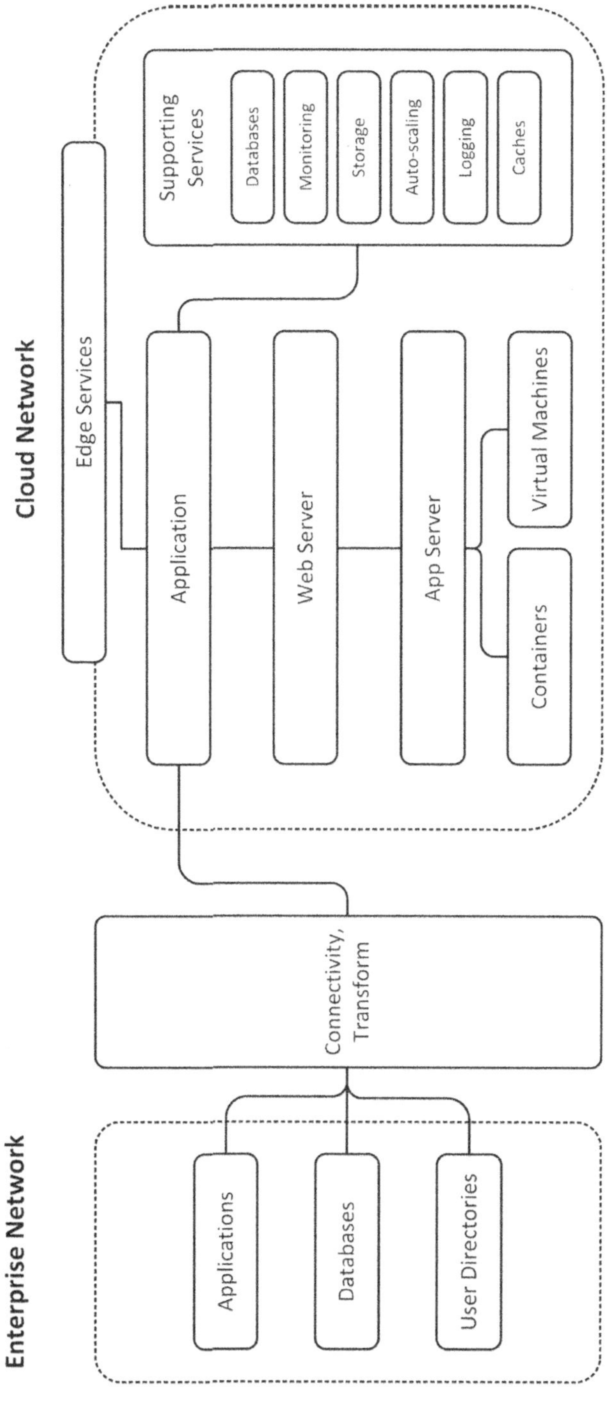

Figure 7: Generic Application Architecture on Cloud

Major/Significant changes in moving a traditional Client-Server architecture app implemented in enterprise datacenter to the Cloud are as following:

1. Thick clients have lost their relevance on the cloud in providing the user interface. The user interface client for cloud-based applications is the browser, which has become universal now. The client includes not only the user interface but also the application's programming interfaces. Of course, there can be specialized clients as well, but those are used to access the application's programming interfaces and not the user interface. All the clients access the application through one or more Uniform Resource Locators or URLs, which provide the web addresses of various resources of the application.

2. The client has also become standardized. The architects now are concerned about keeping the client loads to be minimal possible simply because the browser provides a thin layer of computing. Also, there are standards from W3C (World Wide Web Consortium), which guide on what are the dos and don'ts for an application for building and rendering the web pages, especially when it comes to accessing the machine resources through which the browser is invoked.

3. Since it is universal, the browser is now becoming more powerful in terms of features it provides. It has led to breakthroughs in the traditional web application software that earlier used to process the business logic only on the server. Browser is becoming more and more potent in its ability to execute scripts. It has given way to something called isomorphic applications that carry the scripts that can run both on the server as well as the client, i.e., browser. It has advantages - distribution of a load of execution from just the server to the client, and improvement of search engine optimization features.

4. Since the client is universal now, the operations team is relieved from maintaining the client versions across the application's user community.

5. Server configurations in cloud environments have become a matter of keeping settings in something called manifests. Cloud platforms detect such settings while deploying the application, and the servers or the execution environments are provisioned as per the desired configurations. It has led to the abstraction of all infrastructure provisioning work from developers.

6. Cloud provides additional benefits of providing the latest versions of all popular runtimes. Developers are no more responsible for downloading dependencies, and it's the cloud platform's responsibility to ensure that the required dependencies are downloaded and made available to the application.

7. Configurations like connection pooling and RPC threading are driven by settings rather than maintaining those in XML files of the application server's configuration, which were generally not available to a developer in client-facing environments.

8. Cloud also provides a lot of supporting services to the application developers that can enhance the features of the applications. Developers need not be concerned anymore about writing codes or using external libraries to implement such features. For example, authentication, database, file storage services for the application are readily available in most of the clouds.

9. All the services, including the database, are now invoked on the HTTP layer with additional benefits of TLS that also standardizes the use of services for the applications. JDBC

and ODBC connectivity remain available on the cloud, but rather than connecting through native or OLEDB/ADODB providers, apps now connect through HTTP providers.

10. Security is a signicant consideration in the cloud. Identity management makes the use of federation, which utilizes cloud-based identity management systems enabling single sign-on. Cloud providers also provide additional levels of security by giving the certificate and key-store services. While network security, physical security, and device security are responsibilities of cloud providers, application security is still implemented by the application team. VPNs can be set up to access an enterprise network from the cloud.

11. Cloud platform provisions single virtual execution environment that includes both the app and web server (merged into one) during the deployment of the application, and the server is no more required to be provisioned before deploying the application.

12. To utilize the full features of the cloud, applications need to be re-architected to make them more loosely coupled. In a traditional app, items like database location, network connections to access the database, and the various points of interoperability with operating systems, middleware, and other tools are either coded or dependent on such links and resources being local. In the cloud, however, the objective is to break away from this as cloud apps must be ready to access whatever is needed wherever it is at. Such applications are then known as native to cloud or born in the cloud or designed for the cloud.

As we can see from the above, the cloud has led to standardizations on how to architect, design, build, and deploy the applications on the cloud. Later on, we will discuss the principles that govern the designing and building of the apps on the cloud. This approach has led the enterprises to look for the same standardizations even for the applications meant to be or remain deployed within the enterprise datacenter as we believe that enterprises will eventually also implement private cloud within their datacenter.

The highest level of cloud nativity is microservices architecture and API first design. From that perspective, the application architecture in the cloud can also be depicted below. It is discussed in more detail in the section, "Microservices".

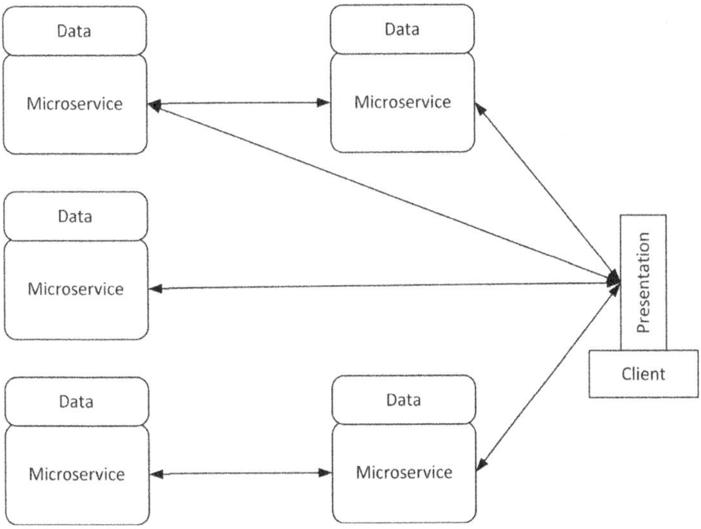

Figure 8: Cloud Native Application Architecture

This book is written to describe this particular architecture, but it is essential to touch the levels of cloud and its value for applications.

2.4.2 IaaS - What is it suitable for?

Infrastructure as a service is your virtual machine in the cloud. Depending upon the contract with your cloud provider, you may manage that virtual machine yourself or choose the cloud provider (or even a third party) to accomplish that. Typical management activities are maintenance at OS levels such as patch and OS resource administration. IaaS is useful for getting virtually limitless scalability and agility. And in most cases, it can save the cost also. Since it is paid by use, it eliminates the CAPEX and transfers the budget to OPEX as it provides data center infrastructures, such as compute, storage, networking, and networking services. Enterprises still need to manage applications, data, runtime, middleware, and OSes. Service providers manage virtualization, servers, hard drives, storage, and networking. However, many IaaS providers have started to offer databases, messaging queues, and other services above the virtualization layer as well, which has led to the coinage of the term IaaS+.

IaaS and Application Architecture

To use IaaS, applications can be migrated to the cloud as a whole unit. There is no redesigning and is, therefore, less costly to relocate. But if the app is not redesigned to optimize it for cloud or make less resource-intensive, the running cost will quickly outweigh the migration cost.

To migrate an application to an IaaS, the requirements are lower. The entire software is migrated. The application code, along with the operating system, is migrated to the cloud. The application is packaged in a full software stack as one or more virtual machine (VM) images. The images can then be copied into the cloud service and provisioned there as virtual machines. The application, however, should still not be dependent on:

1. Any device driver as those may not be supported on the IaaS
2. MAC addresses as the machines are virtual
3. Locally hosted resources

2.4.3 PaaS - What value it delivers

When you add additional resources for development and deployment on the top of IaaS, then it becomes PaaS - Platform as a service. PaaS provides a framework that the enterprise developers can use to build upon or develop applications. It makes the development, and deployment of applications easier, with the flexibility of frameworks, tools, and runtimes while still providing standard application management, platform services such as messaging and caching, and cloud architecture patterns. Service providers manage OSes, virtualization, servers, storage, networking, and the PaaS platform. In a traditional development project, engineers would need middleware, development tools, database management systems, and more, which are provided by the PaaS platform. Developers, however, manage the applications and data.

PaaS platform is designed to offer configuration options, hybrid cloud features, monitoring policy controls, varied storage options, audits and certifications, a host of services to choose from, deployment options, hosting options, security controls, testing tools, reliability, and auto-scaling. It is characterized by enablement through self-service, automation, quotas for consumption control, and programmable access in order to support the building, testing, deploying, managing, and updating of the application.
One of the significant benefits of PaaS is its ability to improve a developer's productivity. PaaS can deliver business agility by enabling rapid development with faster and more frequent delivery of functionality.

PaaS and Application architecture

For an application to fully utilize PaaS, it should meet the following requirements:

1. The application should use one or more runtime environments available on the target PaaS. Few PaaS allow bringing your runtime, but to keep away the responsibility of making available the latest runtime and other dependencies, it is always desired to use the runtimes that are available on the target PaaS environment.
2. Developer only has to be concerned with the application components and data. There should be no dependency on OS, and application should be able to utilize middleware and other services like database and file storage as a loosely coupled service.
3. The application should be able to utilize the execution configurations set through the PaaS environment.
4. The application should be structured appropriately to take advantage of scalable cloud resources, e.g., multiple processors or multiple machines for execution in parallel.
5. Locations of services like database, file storage should not be coded inside, and the application should be able to utilize them as an externally available service.
6. Application dependencies should not be coded inside.
7. Application processes should not persist the data within the application memory.

2.4.4 SaaS- The modern business model

Software as a Service (SaaS) is the de-facto business model for new entrepreneurs. In this business model, the user, rather than paying for the software itself, pays for using it. Users are authorized to use it for the time the software use is paid for. SaaS brings in multiple benefits such as reduced time to business benefits realization, immediate availability of new releases and upgrades at no cost, easy to use and perform proof of concepts, and scalability as well as integration. SaaS provides applications as a service that is managed by the service provider and whose interface is accessed by the enterprise users. SaaS applications are run from a web browser, and there is no need to install and run applications on individual computers. Service providers manage everything - application, runtime, data, middleware, OSes, virtualization, servers, storage, and networking.

SaaS and Application architecture

Enterprises, who subscribe to SaaS do not care about the application architecture except for integration. With the availability of iPaaS, even that is virtually eliminated. All they need to care about is ensuring the availability of the application.

SaaS provider considerations for application architecture, on the other hand, are even more critical as they need to take care of applications' scalability, availability, performance, and security. And because of the pay by use model, metering and billing are essential. Noting that there will be billing complexity because of a variety of billing models, the architecting for the instrumentation needs also becomes critical.

In case of the enterprise as a provider to an internal customer, the application architecture will be essential but not as much as for a SaaS business provider because billing and chargeback would be a simple use case of predicting resource and scalability requirements and also the upper cap on resources and scalability will always be predictable.

3 EMERGING ENTERPRISE STRATEGY: PRODUCT & PLATFORM

To become an agile technology organization and in turn be able to create a strategic differentiation through faster delivery of new capabilities and innovations for disruptive business models, modern enterprises are changing their application development strategy. They are now adopting a products and platform approach that delivers high quality, high-value functionality, and associated services to the business. Agile and DevOps are essential concepts that bring in the transformation to continuously and quickly produce high quality and secure software. The product and platform approach accelerates the development of new business capabilities that are continuously customizable and scalable. It is the driving force for the shift from a project-centric mode to a faster, more agile product-and-platform-based delivery model and enables us to deliver value faster and more often.

A "product" is a commercial offering that brings value to a consumer, customer, or business and consists of a set of systems owned by a team and is exposed as an application or a set of application programming interfaces, APIs. An end-user facing application providing business capabilities delivers value and continues to evolve. Products can be changed without altering the underlying business capability. A product has a life cycle, from conception to being decommissioned. An application software becomes a product when you deliver the same code to multiple "customers" and manage throughout its lifecycle. So, the question is - can an application software for an enterprise become a product? My answer would be yes if you build it in the same way as if there are multiple customers. Noting that the application solution for one customer alone is complicated, so the making of the product for various customers should even be more complicated. Not really when you consider the mindset of the customer. A customer for a software product adjusts the requirements to fit into the software product, but for a solution, the product needs to be tailored to meet the demand of a customer, and thus, it loses its fundamental tenet of being a product. Standardization is the key to the product, while customization is the key to the solution.

A "platform" enables one or more products by providing an underlying base technology, standard services, and modular component. Platforms bring together an interoperable set of Services to develop applications. Services-first versus applications-first is the main attribute of a loosely coupled, interoperable platform. The platform is founded based on a principle that enables freedom within a framework allowing utilization of the right solution for each product, as well as right-size for each client, region, and function. The platform design is driven by advanced architecture principles and based on state-of-the-art cloud technologies to enable agility, cost efficiency, and sustainability.

Benefits of Product & Platform approach in enterprise are:

- Accelerate development of enterprise solutions on the platform.
- Possibility to enable continuous delivery for products. Standardized architecture for products
- Drive automation for scale and efficiency
- Engineer for high availability, self-healing, and anti-fragile approaches
- Utilize a self-service ecosystem
- Leverage elasticity to right-size infrastructure based on demand
- Possibility to embrace mobility and responsive design faster, if supported by the platform.
- Create a high-performance engineering culture with right-sized pods, continuous improvisation, and collaboration.
- Adopt security-first principles to safeguard enterprise data and privacy
- Deliver an engaging, and seamless user experience if the platform offers the user interface designer tool.
- Expand competitive advantage by leveraging innovative solutions and emerging technologies that are provided by the platform.

Building application on a platform

The platform has a comprehensive definition and different levels of abstraction. Popular cloud provider PaaS offering includes universal components and services such as development tools (CI/CD, ATF, etc.), database management, business analytics, runtime, and a catalog of third-party services, but these are the basics offered by any platform of today. A product builder will use development toolset and different framework and programming language to build a product that can run on this native platform or can be deployed on other platforms with the required run time environment. A cloud provider platform can be enriched with additional services as an extra layer. These services would be standard functionalities that are usually required for most of the business applications, for example, virtual assistant, bulletin board, shopping cart, access control, and so on. These services are usable for products to incorporate if built on the platform.

3.1 Product Management

Product vs. Solution

Typically, enterprise applications are built as a solution. It is essential to understand the difference between the product and the solution. Products are made to solve most problems of most customers (rather than solving every problem of every customer). Application solutions in an enterprise are focusing on solving every problem of a single customer. Products are used to implement a customized solution that is specific to the customer. Over some time, products get enriched with more and more capabilities, but no product will ever be a ready-made solution.

Single codebase - Multiple deployments: Codebase is the collection of source code that forms a release. A codebase is stored in a source control repository in a version control system. The codebase is the complete source code required to maintain application functionality or the implementation of that source code. A codebase can be monolithic or distributed depending upon the component, and the repository is single or distributed. It is the most critical aspect of the codebase. For example, the Linux kernel is architecturally a single monolithic kernel, but it consists of separate binaries (loadable components) and is developed in multiple distributed repositories. A product may have multiple releases, and each release may have incremental difference with the base release, yet the codebase is deemed to be the same codebase- the original baselined the first release. The codebase is the very first approach in 12-factor app design.

Release management and Codebase Management: The development team will encounter more significant problems as the codebase becomes larger. Therefore, a large project will require suitable source code repository, systems, and discipline for communication between developers. Release management is different than codebase management. Release management for a product makes the specific version of the product available to a limited (restricted or early release) or to all users (General release). In the context of enterprise application, a release also includes deployment.

Specific business problem vs. general-purpose problem area: Enterprise applications are built to solve a particular enterprise business problem. Product companies, on the other hand, pick up a generic problem and create a product that can solve that problem for most of the customers. Each customer may use it differently and, at times, adjust some of the requirements to use the products.

Opensource and security compliance vs. license management: It is ubiquitous to use open source for the product or the enterprise application. By doing so, you are exposing yourself to the security, license compliance, and code quality risks that come with the use of an open-source. The kind of exposure for building and using an application within an enterprise vs. the same for a product is significantly different. When creating and running an application within the enterprise, you are not selling licenses, but when you are delivering a product to external customers, you are granting the permit, and this changes the way open source licensing terms work.

Internal customer vs. external customer

Internal customers are a kind of captive customers, and external customers are not. Gaining a captive customer is considered to be lucrative. Being a captive customer is a bad feeling, especially when the product and service are not of good quality. It is vital to avoid making your customers feel captive. And the very first thing that you should do is to ensure that the quality of your product and service is never below standards. The application management approach is usually built for internal customers, and a product management approach is developed for external customers. Adopting the latter approach for internal customers will automatically change the mindset and avoid internal customer feel as captive.

3.1.1 Product management

Broader responsibilities associated with product management are as following:

1. Market Research on Customers and Prospects
2. Industry Analysis
3. Competitor Analysis
4. Competitive Landscape and product positioning
5. Product comparisons
6. GTM Plan
7. Sales and marketing support

8. Product requirement management
9. Aggregating requirements from domains
10. Validating product requirements
11. Product release management
12. Product collateral management
13. Demo & Sandbox process
14. Managing IP Compliance
15. Product Validation testing
16. Product pricing and licensing strategy

3.1.2 Product Management Lifecycle

How an engagement lifecycle maps with the product lifecycle?

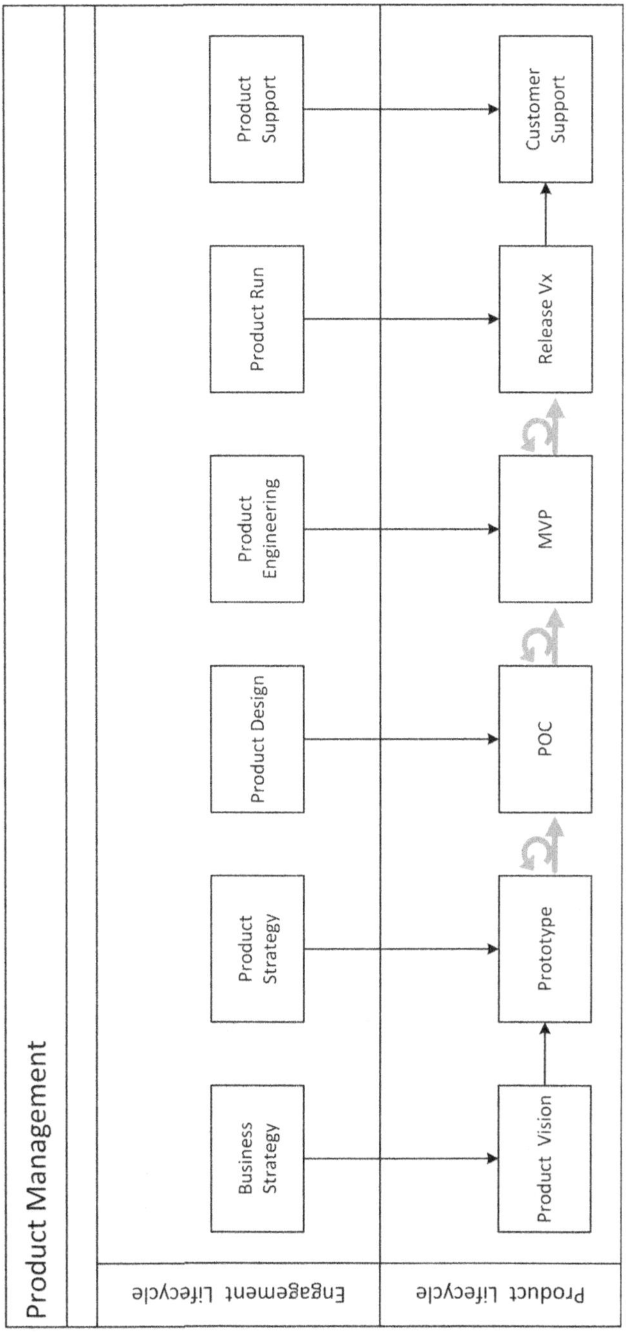

Figure 9: Product Management and Engagement Model

3.1.3 Product-Centric mindset

Focus on Value

Consumer utility and experience is at the center of the value proposition. User experience is a sum of all parameters or user-facing attributes of a service, but in the context of software design, the user experience focuses on how an application user will interact with the application. When a developer is building an application for an enterprise, he will focus on how an employee will interact, and most often, a corporate has a standard and approved set of end-user devices to communicate. However, for a product build, the users are external and unknown and can interact with any standard device available in the open market. When you think from the software application perspective, software engineering is on the top of the mind. Codes are intangible for the end customer, but the product is not. The product thinking will hide the intangibility and bring the user experience to the front.

Start Small Build Fast

MVP or minimum viable product allows you to start small and get the initial market test, user feedback test, and viability of the product much faster because of a reduced time to market — the product's position is based on vision and roadmap rather than the features and functions that are available today. In an enterprise application solution, it is also a partially applicable concept even though you are not selling a product within the organization, but you are allowing users to obtain little benefit much earlier than the usual time. The ability to collect instant feedback from potential users is the most significant advantage of MVP.

Experiment and Experimental Design

While developing a product from scratch, experimenting refers to describe our actions when we are testing or trying out something new, for example, experimenting with a new open-source or experimenting with a different framework. In such situations, the experimentation is performed unwittingly in a somewhat ad hoc or uncontrolled manner. In experimental design, what to experiment and what not should be the matter of a qualified approach. If adopted with a well-qualified approach, product design and delivery must result in better with less wastage of time. The experimental design is more a matter of POC (proof of concept) rather than prototyping.

Design Thinking

Thinking itself is a high-value skill that is difficult to find these days in the society that is overwhelmed by social media, and social media does not create social intelligence. Likewise, the design thinking for the product is also a high-value skill for product building organizations that is not easy to find because the technology by itself does not create thinking.

Design thinking is not only an aptitude but also a process to understand users, challenge assumptions, redefine problems, and create an innovative product. Among many, the one challenge that stands out is the one that talks about design for user experience. It is quite easy for us to illustrate this with an example of Apple's 3D Touch.

A few years ago, on iPhone 6, Apple had introduced an entirely new way with which users can interact with their phones. For the first time, the iPhone has senses that tells it how much pressure we are applying to the screen. In addition to the already familiar multi-touch gestures such as tap, swipe, and pinch, 3D Touch introduces 'peek' and 'pop'. It adds a new dimension to the functional experience of using an iPhone. It also makes the iPhone respond with subtle taps. It means that not only will we be able to see what a press can do, but we will also be able to feel it. 3D Touch is one of the most innovative features to appear on a mobile phone touchscreen. 3D Touch is not just a new feature but is a fundamental change in the way we have been physically interacting with our devices. 3D Touch starts with the idea of estimating the force applied on a thin device. From a traditional designer's perspective, it would just be a matter of designing something to detect any force applied to the device. Had that been the case, the designer would have failed to deliver overall experience because the user experience is always beyond the force they apply on the device. To give a positive user experience, the designer will need to design a device that senses the intent of the user rather than design one that detects or estimates the force applied. That would require the ability to read the users' minds. That would also mean considering the user's environment and situation. For instance, the user might be using his / her thumb or finger to access the device features, or might be emotional at the moment, or might be walking, or just relaxing on a couch. All these scenarios do not affect the intent. However, they do change what a sensor inside the thin iPhone 6 sees. Undeniably, there are several design-only challenges to deal with. That said, it wouldn't be appropriate to sideline the importance of capturing the user intent. It adds complexities to the component design, which will lead to further intent-related challenges.

Here, a sensor cannot be a simple transducer. It should be combined with an accelerometer to nullify the effect of gravity. Again, nullify here means adding or subtracting the force, depending upon the direction of the motion. Similarly, detecting whether the user was touching the screen with his/her thumb or with his/her other fingers is vital to interpret the force. This led

Apple to fuse the accelerometer in the sensor to detect the nature of interaction and added algorithms. This was one of those things that proved that if we fail to get it right, nothing built upon it will work. Apple did get it right, and hence stood out amongst all its competitors and continues to maintain its lead in innovation.

Rapid Prototyping

Rapid prototyping has been very common in physical product build but very well applicable in software products as well. Prototyping is a step next to POC (Proof of Concept). While the POC proves the feasibility of a product or feature, the prototype demonstrates how it will work. Prototyping is the design verification phase of product development because it demonstrates or proves the design. Prototyping provides an opportunity to make new changes, and thus save time and cost.

Value pyramid

In the value pyramid, from an idea to the software product, the idea commands the highest value. The idea is the beginning of innovation though every idea cannot be an innovation or convertible into a product that can be commercialized. When we keep an idea's value factor at the highest level, we mean it for a qualified idea, not just an idea.

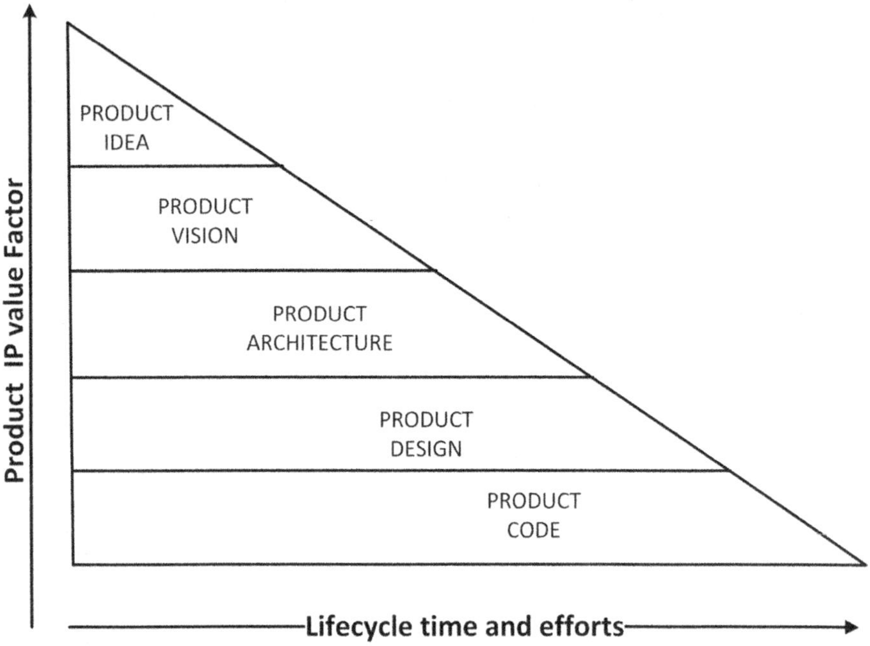

Figure 10: Product Value Factor Pyramid

If a brilliant idea is not taken to the market in time, then the value is diminished as the cost of lost opportunity matters. Even though the idea has the highest value in the pyramid, it also has the highest risk of copying. Ideas cannot be patented, but the invention can be, and for that, the invention itself has to be produced using the idea. The idea is the point of beginning and must be supported by the vision it carries for the realization of value in a sustained manner when productized. That is where the roadmap comes. Once the idea and vision are crystal clear, architecture is developed that will be able to materialize the idea in the product's entire lifespan. For a software product, it may not be viable, but the attempt should be made for a future proof architecture. Till this point of time in the value chain, it is a matter of strategy as the Architecture faces towards strategy, structure, and purpose, and is abstract. Design faces implementation, and practice, and is concrete. Architecture is a plan for the construction of something. Design is a plan to create something. Hence design is the beginning point of execution that ends with the build. Engineering is the bridge that takes you from architecture to design. As we go down in the value factor, the lifecycle time and efforts for that activity increases. Also, the skill value declines, yet the skill availability increases.

Learn and Evolve

The idea to POC is one phase where you learn and evolve to bring in a viable shape to the idea in the form of a product. But learning and evolving continues for further refinement and enhancement of the product. Learn and evolve is the philosophy that thrives on building better and better products with every generation. If you are thinking and working with a product mindset, then you will internally trigger the ongoing development. However, if you are thinking of application development, then you will wait for some external event or person to trigger the development for betterment. In other words, the product mindset drives continuous refinement.

3.2 Application Management

In the 1990s, application management as a discipline started gaining ground in the enterprise IT, and industry-standard frameworks began gaining popularity. Going through the application management phases of a generic application management framework, as we see below, it is evident that the mindset is technical. Application as a product came much later in the industry - long after the business applications came into existence and in use. Therefore, the root of the mindset created with the software engineering discipline is older than the recognition of application as a product.

1. Requirements and Requirement management
    a. Functional Requirements
    b. Non-Functional Requirements
    c. Usability Requirements
    d. Testing Requirements
2. Architect and Design
    a. Architecture
    b. Design for manageability
    c. Managing Design Trade off
3. Build
    a. Coding convention
    b. Application framework
    c. Application Instrumentation
4. Deploy
    a. Deployment planning
    b. Application distribution
    c. Deploy
5. Run
    a. Maintenance schedule
    b. Application state information management

Since the proliferation of the Internet and the explosion of the application product market, the recognition of application as a product is evident.

3.3 Building an enterprise application with a product mindset

The application management mindset is the default mindset for every enterprise IT and revolves around the generic framework that we described in the earlier section. Keeping the same goal of the outcome, changing the perspective to product management is the emerging approach.

Product approach in enterprise

It would sound like a strange approach, but it brings in good things. It becomes instrumental in giving up the old way of doing things. It brings in different thinking also. In traditional application development and support, you were acting as and treated as the "order taker". However, with the product management approach, you have an opportunity to position yourself as the thought leader and expert service provider. When you think of building a product, the most critical role -product manager- would take the centerstage. The holistic role of a product manager includes many activities, and in the context of an enterprise environment, several of them, such as product marketing related activities, would become irrelevant. The diagram below represents what activities of a product manager matter if you are building the product for an enterprise.

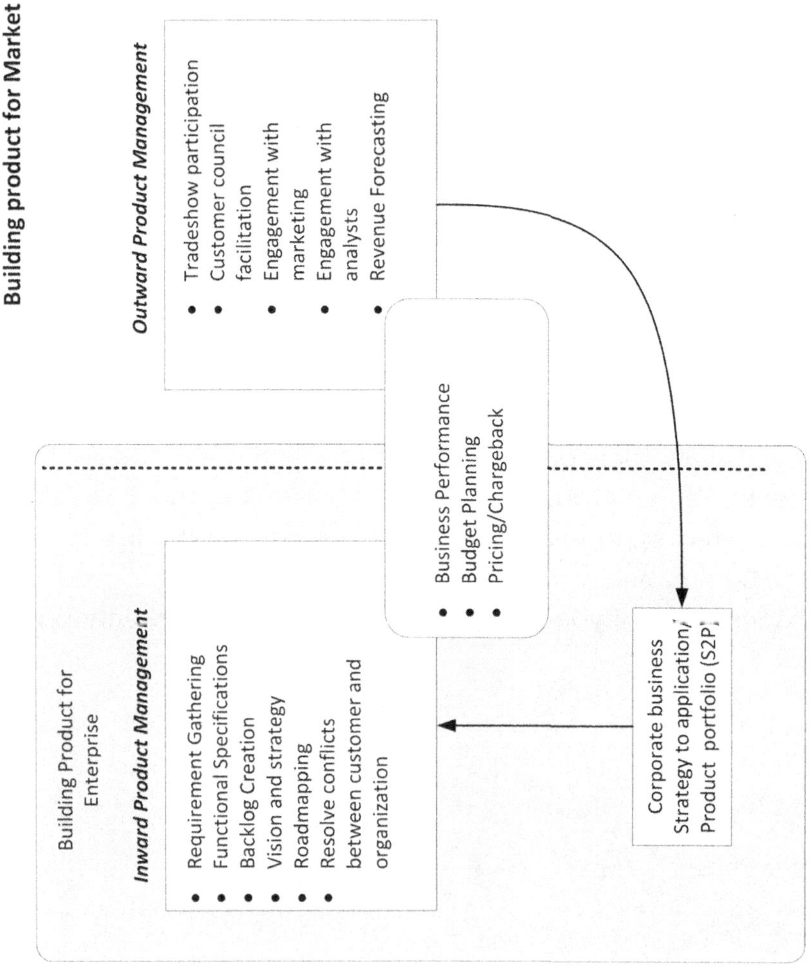

Figure 11: Scope of Product Management in Enterprise

Depending upon the status of IT in the enterprise (whether it is a cost center or a profit center) business performance of the product, budgeting and chargeback will or will not be in the scope of the product manager in the enterprise.

The critical role of the Product Manager in GTM

Outward product management is mostly the goto marketing and its strategy. Tradeshows are an essential part of marketing, and it is not easy to identify the right tradeshow and obtain the full value of participation. Customer council facilitation requires active relationship management and shrewdness. But in the modern marketing world, working with research analysts to position your product is among the most desired and demanding skills that a product manager needs to have. It makes the product manager a critical contributor to marketing and goto market strategy. By the way, you require internal GTM even if you are building the product for the enterprise users. As we mentioned earlier, internal users of your products in the enterprise are a kind of captive customers, and they have no choice, yet you need a goto market strategy for them. The purpose is to keep your product quality high and continue to justify your value in the enterprise and earn self-esteem.

Do you require GTM within Enterprise?

Product management discipline makes an enterprise application like a commercial product. But this is not the only difference. Other differences are:

- Product is built by design thinking while applications are developed by solution thinking.
- The rule of repeatability governs outcome- that is, one code multiple deployments.

Cost related to building Enterprise App and product

CN apps and products are likely to be more expensive but deliver a higher level of ROI. The commercial is not in the scope of the book, but there is a general misunderstanding of the myth of falling prices for technology. Hardware price is falling, but the software is increasingly getting resource-hungry, so the net result is a higher cost of the outcome.

IT people are well versed in Moore's law. It is the observation made by Gordon Moore, co-founder of Intel Corporation more than 50 years ago (in 1965 to be exact), that the number of transistors per square inch on integrated circuits would be doubled every year since the integrated circuit was invented. That speaks about the progress in the technology, but the appetite for the processing power is also growing, probably at a faster rate. It is the observation of C.N. Parkinson, a British political analyst, and a historian, which was published in 1955. It states that the work expands to fill in the time available for its completion. The implication is that no matter how extensive your resources, the demands on them will grow to ensure they are depleted. In application development, I see the influence of Parkinson's law. In DevOps, the number of stories in a sprint does grow, and most of the time, some of the stories are pushed to the next sprint. One of the methods to deal with the phenomenon of Parkinson's law is to use Parkinson's law of triviality, and that is another observation that people tend to devote a significant amount of time to unimportant details while essential tasks are not getting the time they require. The law goes beyond. The expansion crosses the boundary of resources, and then the resources are pulled in from the back door.

An example of this is the self-serving processes in Windows operating system. The relative computing resources available to a user are declining as the operating system services grew resource hungry. In Windows 95, the number of self-service processes was 19, and that has grown to over 100 in Windows 10!

Windows 3.x was one of the earliest OS that had a graphical user interface that made it look fancy, path-breaking, and hugely popular. It required at least 1 MB of memory with 8 MB of hard disk space and could access a maximum of 16 MB, which was considered an awful memory back in the early 1990s when it was released.

Another interesting fact is about NASA's Apollo 11 mission. The computers that were part of the mission, controlled the various systems, including the communications and the power systems. These computers are reported to have run on a far less computing power than what we have today on our mobile phones. Unverified facts suggest that the memory was 4 KB, storage was 32 KB, and the processor was 150 times less potent than what few modern-day mobile phones have. Have we not progressed from what we could achieve through the system configuration back in 1969 to what we need today to send jokes, messages, and media snippets from our mobile phones?

3.4 MVP- The Foundation of Building the Product

Definition of MVP

A minimum viable product (MVP) is a product with just enough functionality to convince early customers that it provides value and to provide feedback for further product development. In lean product development, the minimum viable product or MVP is a part of strategy to avoid building products that customers do not need or want by maximizing our learning of what is valuable to the customer. MVP is more a part of time to market strategy rather than a development strategy, although, in today's world, MVP is invariably associated with DevOps and agile methodologies.

The right size of MVP

The art is in developing or sizing MVP in the "Goldilocks" zone-that is, you are not developing more or developing less, but just right to validate your product assumptions with an MVP. The assumptions that you may want to test with MVP are:

1. The purposefulness of the product- The product is fit for the

purpose it is built.

2. The usefulness of the product - the product is fit for the use of intended users.
3. User Experience- the users are delighted to use the product.

Therefore, the MVP must contain the minimum viable components of all the above three elements.

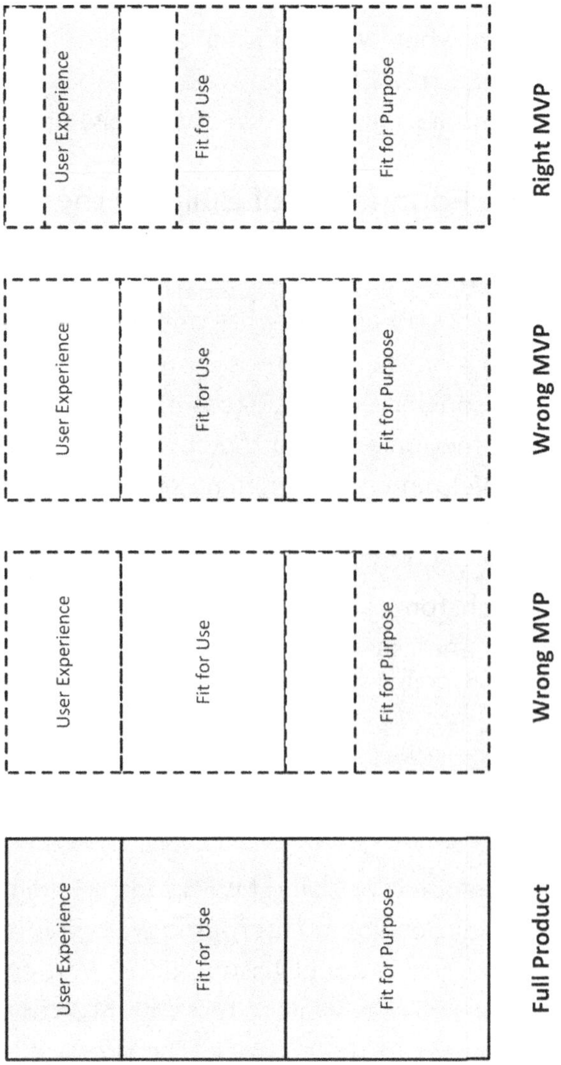

Figure 12: Right Content of MVP

Identify features that users would expect as the core, get user feedback on those in order to finalize the features required to be built in MVP. This will determine the right functionality your product needs to acquire and retain users and hence to establish its feasibility. Over time, the feedback and learnings from MVP help defining the product roadmap and guiding the evolution of the product.

Can MVP ever be correct?

The content of an MVP is subjective. It is a matter of judgment on how much would be sufficient for each element of purpose, use, and user experience to be included in MVP. It depends upon the marketing strategy and the target MVP customers' perception/acceptance. If you are perceived as an established and strong product company with the vision, then you are starting with a favorable position. MVP customer is willing to adjust the requirements based on the MVP usability. However, in an enterprise application scenario, even if you build a product, the MVP size and contents will be dictated by the customer, and you will be expected to adjust your MVP content accordingly.

Why is MVP important?

The Minimum Viable Product enables testing the earliest product in the market conditions with the users for the appropriateness of its features and its performance. The minimum viable product is a product that includes only just enough features to allow the company to release it to the market.

An MVP is a smart way to:

- Release your product to the market in the shortest time.
- Reduce implementation costs.

- Test the demand for your product - before releasing a full-fledged product.
- Avoid failures and loss of capital investment.
- Gain insights into what v/s what does not work.
- Get feedback from customers on the user behavior and preferences.
- Gather and enhance your user base.

MVP is practically the birth of a product. It is like labor before birth that is painful and difficult, but after birth, parents spend most of the effort and time with.

3.5 Agility

Agility, as we all know, is the ability to deliver quickly, but I will also add easily, besides quickly. Agility is among the most glorified words used in the past several years in enterprise IT and, unfortunately, used to pressurize enterprise CIOs unjustly. I do not intend to defend CIOs who are not agile but want to emphasize that the agility concept is not just applicable to IT but to the entire ecosystem and many parts of that is often outside the domain of CIO. The scope of agility, even if it is limited to IT, should be clearly understood before setting any expectation on what benefit it would deliver.

Agility in isolation has no value. For example, if Amazon retailing site allows you to place the order in an agile system and Amazon also routes order to actual supplier quickly, but what it would be good for, if the supplier system is not agile to process the order or even if the shipment is agile, delivery channel is not designed to deliver quickly? Similarly, what is it good for if the server is rapidly provisioned, but the database licenses procurement takes weeks or even if you deploy the application in the automated matter, the setting up of monitoring and control for operations takes months because of internal processes? In other words, being agile is meaningless if the entire ecosystem that delivers the outcome is not agile as well.

3.5.1 Insanity in agility expectations

Bureaucratic enterprise expecting IT agility!!!

The business expects IT to be agile, but is business itself agile? Right, the business has a dependency on IT, but does IT not have a dependence on business? For an enterprise itself to be agile, IT is just one of the many factors. Most of the time, it is the internal and external bureaucracy that makes a barrier towards IT agility. Bureaucracy is the management structure within a company and the way to manage operations according to that structure. Usually, it evolves within large corporations or the government. Though it is formed to help better manage something, it can get too bulky and inefficient, which is characterized by excessive formality and routine required before official action can be taken. An organization is deemed bureaucratic when its policies do not satisfy the customer's situation; that is, the policies and procedures are rigid and applied uniformly across all situations. For example, internal processes to get resources, to get the budget and miscellaneous approvals to start the project. Where is the agility gone for this part of the project? Bureaucracy will take 80% of the total time for the project delivery and then pressurize IT to do a miracle in 20% of the time in the name of agility. Another example that we can easily cite from our experience of service delivery organization is that the business acquisition team spends several months in writing the SOW and contract but expect agility to start next day!

Agility costs money

It is no brainer - not only in IT but in all businesses, speed has a premium and also that agility with security costs significantly more money. If you want to drive at high speed, you should have the right vehicle designed for high speed, skilled driver to drive in high gear, roads built to support high-speed driving. If the entire group wants to operate together at high speed, then everyone should have skills and vehicle that is correctly designed. Even on a freeway, a clueless driver or a slow driver can slow down the entire traffic. The agile methodology relies on the uniform and efficient skills across all the team members because they all need to work synchronously in a sprint. The cost of just one agile developer in the group vs. the cost of the entire agile group is a big difference. For that purpose, agility is not scalable beyond a limit. Even though agility is expensive, it is not a problem because there are buyers who are ready to pay for it. The question for the organization is, are you willing to invest (in being agile) and obtain higher ROI on that investment? Unfortunately, this part of the agility is rarely discussed.

Agility with design quality not only costs more but has conflicts that have the potential to defeat the agility. Design is the root of all quality, and design quality is the value to the customer. A product with poor design will be of low quality even if the quality assurance is confirming the product's adherence to the design. For a software product, how you design the story to produce the desired functional requirement can significantly impact the design quality. For example, a business rule can very quickly be coded and built into the product to deliver the desired outcome, but the same can be designed as a configurable item in a product and, therefore, can provide better value to a wide range of customers. The tradeoff is in the timeline. To design high quality, you need more time (and money as well). Design quality parameters are as following:

1. Feature and Function: Optimal characteristics. Many times overwhelming features become a burden.
2. Usability: Fit for use for the intended purpose and ability of a user to use feature/function.
3. Security: Access. and controls to use the product and associated data.
4. User Interface: Aesthetics of the interface
5. Performance: Ability to deliver the outcome

Designing skills and that too, with multiple dimensions of quality design, is difficult to be right for the first time unless you have brilliant designers.

The inertia of the organization

Any DevOps team will be a part of a larger organization and cannot exist in isolation. It will inherit the inertia of the organization, and that is decided by the overall business efficiency, not just the IT efficiency or the DevOps agility. IT and DevOps depend upon other organization functions like budgeting, vendor management, funding, talent acquisition and talent retention, tools, and tools vendors, and so on. One slow function can impact the entire agility of any IT or DevOps team.

Business lifecycle vs. IT lifecycle

Compare the business lifecycle and IT Lifecycle of any business, for example, a pharmaceutical company launching a drug or an airline Launching a new flight service- a new sector or an insurance company launching a new product. The regulatory approval and planning lifecycle runs in months to years as compared to the IT lifecycle. More often, the inefficiency of the external factors puts unwarranted pressure on the IT or DevOps.

Culture of the organization

Culture is an integrated pattern of value, attitude, practices, goals, beliefs, and behaviors acquired by employees of the organization. It is also inherited from the society, region, and the country. It is directly related to working style and therefore reflects in the product and service offered by the organization. An employee in a highly successful service company will acquire a service-oriented culture. and the work style will focus on adjusting the service according to the customer need. An employee of a product company will have a different working style. If you are building an application for an enterprise, then it is more likely to be made from a service mindset, and that may not be the best way to build a product. Culture can be developed, and accelerated cultural change is possible by inspirational leadership.

Working environment

It is not easy to create an agile island within the landscape of a bureaucratic enterprise and not when the island is integrated with the mainland for all supporting business functions. A standard business function may not work for serving two different work styles. For example, an HR function that is designed to hire service delivery skills, cannot employ creation skills. Not only that, the policy may not support to retain creative abilities.

3.5.2 MVB is the foundation of Agility

The source of bureaucracy is inefficient and ineffective processes (desire to over-control). Also, bureaucracy results from organizational culture or individual personalities and is rooted in fear of being blamed for wrongdoing, which makes employees create evidence of their right actions in the system, which takes time and effort. This behavior also occurs because of a general mistrust for others as well as for the system. Bureaucracy is not entirely negative and has some required advantages such as transparency and openness, explicit norms and rules, predictable outcomes, and defined accountability. Therefore, for agility, we need a minimum of viable bureaucracy (MVB).

What is MVB?

Minimum Viable Bureaucracy is the bureaucracy with the optimal level of controls that allows and empowers taking the risk in making faster decisions. It believes in a governance model that emphasizes right persons taking the decision rather than focusing on the massive oversight system of governance. MVP is highly conducive to agile business. The underlying theme is that individuals make a better decision than the group, assuming that the individual is an expert in his/her domain in which he/she is making a decision.

MVB is not ad hoc: Adhoc is something done for a particular purpose only and purely transaction-based. An adhoc thing is not repetitive. An enterprise may have bureaucracy with the regular instances of adhoc decisions, but that does not make bureaucracy as MVB. MVB is scalable, but adhocness is not. Being ad-hoc in the business is similar to *jugaad* that we have discussed later, and being ad-hoc in the IT is visible almost everywhere in operations of support and run.

3.6 Effort and duration estimates

It is critical to identify the early customers, and their most pressing needs to assume the features required in the MVP. It is essential to cross-verify and agree with the enterprise stakeholders and, if possible, early customers on the assumptions of necessary features.

When we travel by air, how do you calculate the travel duration? Is this the flying time?

Airline time calculation, as published in the time-table, includes the flying time (wheels up to touch down duration) and average taxing time both ways. But that is not the entire travel time for you. Airport time calculation will include checking in time for passenger and baggage, security check time, boarding time, deplaning time, and baggage retrieval time. Your travel time calculation will also include ground transportations time both ways -that is- starting from a point like Home/Office/Hotel to the departure airport and from arrival airport to a destination point like Home/Office/Hotel.

A one hour flying time (wheel up to touch down) can translate into more than 3 hours if everything is right. But, adding the margins like traffic jams, security check delay, taxing time on tarmac will require at least 4- 5 hours in your reliable plan. A seasoned traveler can reduce that total time, but a conservative traveler would add the margin to cover all the possibilities and may quote 6-7 hours.

Likewise, when we are building MVP, the duration is the sum of many ignored parts. Let us now look at the aspects that cause the minimum viable product to not release within the expected timelines.

1. The decision on the inclusion of security and performance tests - Security and performance tests usually throw a lot of issues and vulnerabilities. It takes a considerable effort to fix those

issues and vulnerabilities. Often, it is overlooked during the finalization of scope and is an after-thought just before the release. Therefore, the decision on inclusion is a critical factor in estimating the duration.

2. You are including non-value adding features unless specifically required to be included in MVP. Examples are - building accessibility features on each screen, user-driven themes of the application, multi-factor authentication mechanism, etc.

3. You are considering elaborate documentation as a part of MVP. Instead of adding more documentation, ideas could be wireframed and tried by writing code and testing.

4. You are making the epic attempt to define the method of delivering the outcome rather than the result itself.

5. Not trying multiple options for an idea and not weighing in possibilities before deciding upon one of those.

6. You are not deciding on the optimal level of tolerance on security vulnerabilities and defects.

7. Micromanagement of team - The key is to have excellent developers. Good developers like to be left alone, and autonomy leads to increased responsibility. If micro-managed, developers do not feel empowered to determine the way they need to take to complete the work and hence achieve the overall goals.

8. Imbalanced team - Team should be multi-disciplined in various aspects to be self-sufficient in building, testing, and delivering the MVP.

9. Imbalances in the system - A delicate balance has to be struck between flexibility and maintainability, efficiency, and responsiveness of the application. Too much focus on one aspect at the cost of others renders the system inconsistent and compromised integrity.

10. Targeting the components and not the system - One needs to focus on functionalities and not the whole system to be delivered as the minimum viable product. The product consists of interacting components and not just the elements working in isolation.

11. Not avoiding feature creeps.

4 CLOUD NATIVE

The definition of native-ness is something designed for or built into a given system. Historically it was denoting the language associated with a given processor, computer, or compiler, and programs written in it could be applied to the broader environment. And by this definition, Cloud Native application means an application designed and built to run in any cloud. Does it mean that buying a virtual machine, designing, and creating even a monolithic application in the cloud will make it a Cloud Native application? Technically yes, and we have explained later with the degree of cloud nativity. However, the true potential of Cloud Native is realized only with specific architectural criteria. Cloud Native applications are by design infrastructure agnostic, which means that they are decoupled from the infrastructure and are free to move when required.

It is worthwhile to mention that the meaning of "Cloud Native" is different for different people. According to a recent article in Forbes, being Cloud Native describes strategies, people, teams, and companies to "get" the cloud to use it for maximum utility. Others use it to describe an approach to building, deploying, and managing things in a cloud computing environment. Being Cloud Native helps companies think about innovating to maximum advantage. Too often, though, it creates misunderstanding and exclusion. "Native" suggests difference from what was born elsewhere but now being considered for cloud. Perhaps a term like "cloud-optimized" is a better way to express what we're talking about when we talk about "Cloud Native," but it's hard to change the terminology.

Nevertheless, in the context of our book, we mean Cloud Native as a qualification for software application for the degree of cloud nativity, or someone can also term it as cloud optimization. We believe four major factors define the Cloud Native application, and these are DevOps, CI/CD, Microservices, and Containers. These are described in detail in subsequent sections.

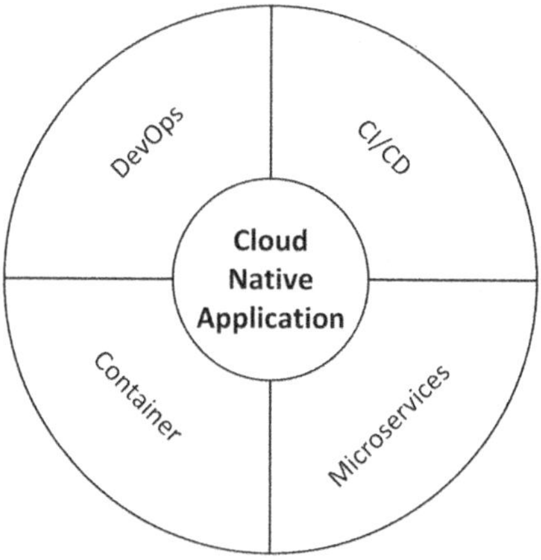

- DevOps: Agile methodology to build and run applications
- CI/CD: Capability to deliver (and optionally deploy) application almost continuously
- Microserrvice: Independent modular component of an application focused for specific function and used through API calls
- Container: Application package with its dependencies build to run on virtualized OS

Figure 13: Essential elements of a Cloud Native Application

Let us discuss these elements in subsequent sections.

4.1 DevOps

Most of the DevOps depictions are presented around the eight activities, namely Plan, Code, Build, Test, Release, Deploy, Run, and Monitor. Multiple representations are floating around in various forums on the Internet, and they vary in semantics and the importance of individual activities. Nevertheless, none of them disagree that DevOps is the software development methodology characterized by the following three fundamental things:

1. Combined working of development and operation teams, including the business stakeholder, to design, to develop, and to support the deployments.
2. Frequent small/incremental releases
3. A very high degree of automation in build test and deploy

What Improvements are brought in by DevOps?

1. Product Acceptance: Because continual participation of business makes the product more relevant.
2. Environment Consistency: Because of the rapid provisioning of an environment with little or no differences between them.
3. Delivery Process Speed: Because of the agile approach.
4. More Focus: DevOps brings in more focus on real work and reduce time spent on creating supporting documentation work such as status report and manual procedural work.
5. Better documentation: Artifacts are created in the system as you do the task assigned to various participants in the DevOps team such as Product Manager, Developer, Tester, etc.

Where is Architect in DevOps?

While DevOps and agility (and related investments) are heavily focused on adding the features and building the new product around features and functions, it would be a wrong approach to limit the efforts in designing the system reliability, scalability, and efficient to "good enough" level. Architecture and design are not visible to customers, but they form the foundation of software

visible to customers, but they form the foundation of software engineering. It is also a wrong notion that the software "stabilized" in production requires virtually no attention from the architect.

However, the architectural review will be necessitated in certain situations like:

1. need for a change to meet enhanced performance, availability, and security-related requirements from the user community
2. need to migrate the application to another cloud
3. there is a change in the supporting services
4. there is a need to alter the security mechanism which is an integral part of the architecture
5. there is a change required in a cross-cutting application process
6. there is a change needed in the way application consumes any of the supporting services

End to End Cycle and Roles in DevOps

The picture below will help to design the full functional organization to build and run the Cloud Native application. The product manager role has already been discussed in detail earlier, it would be essential and to gain an understanding of how it interacts with other functions.

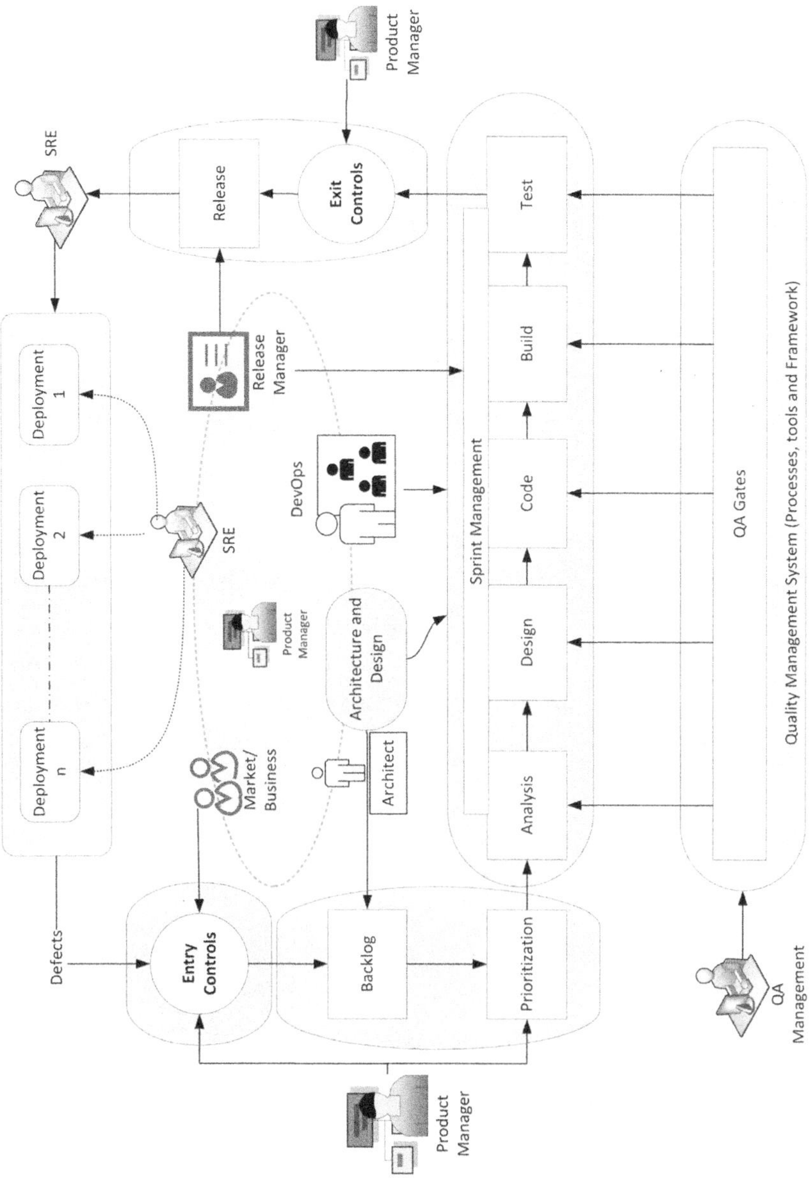

Figure 14: DevOps Roles with product Lifecycle Considerations

The product manager has a vital role in entry and exit control in the product development lifecycle. While the market feedback (or business functions in the enterprise) will flood the user stories, acceptance and prioritization remain with the product manager. Similarly, the developed product's conformance to the user story is also verified by the product manager as a step-in exit control before it is released.

4.1.1 The idea to product- Process perspective

For turning anything to an output, a process is required. The process defines the task, sequence, and roles to perform tasks. Process diagrams are very helpful in establishing an understanding of who, when, do what, and for doing that who will provide input and who will use the output of the task. This understanding will help to do efficient work within the team and collaboration among the team members. Even though DevOps is deemed to be technical work, there is a business process behind it. The idea to product is input to output conversion, and we are breaking it into two different processes.

Idea to MVP

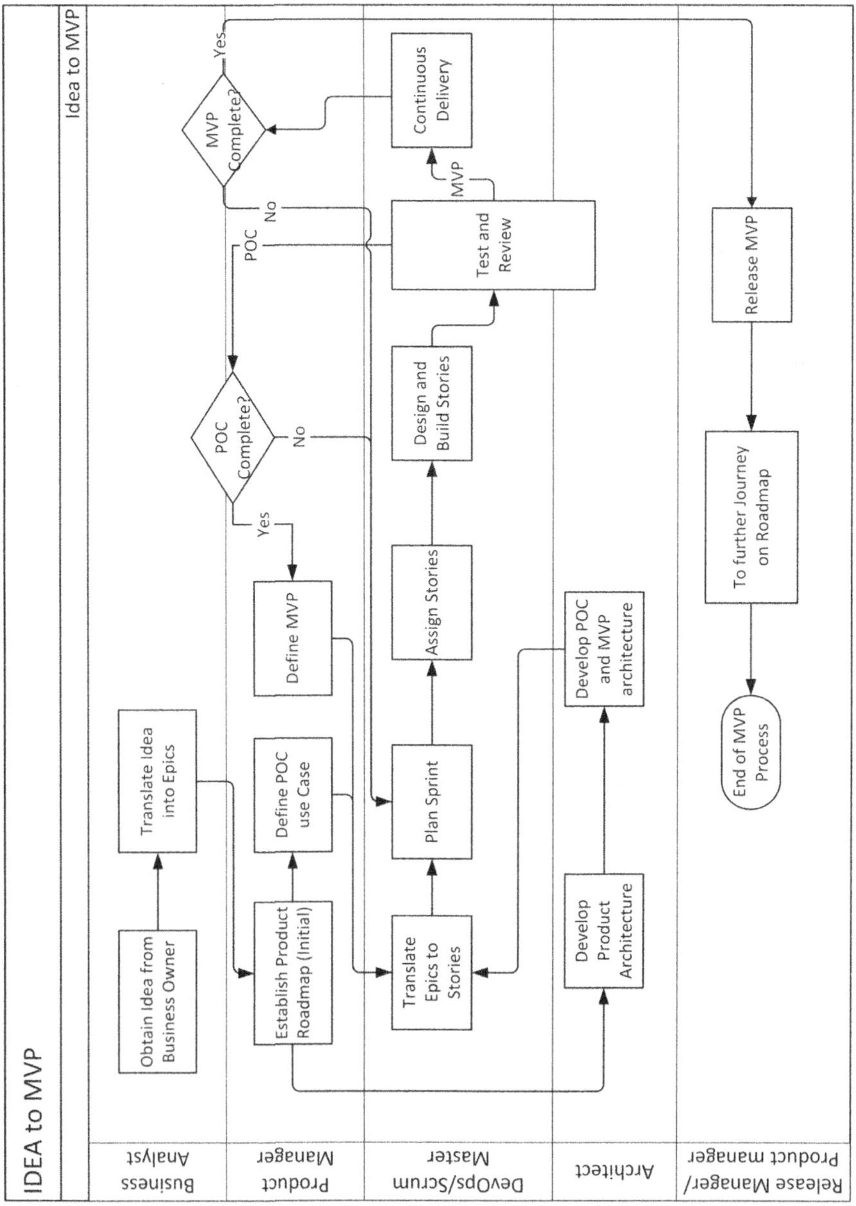

Figure 15: Idea to MVP Process Perspective

Product Roadmap Ongoing Journey

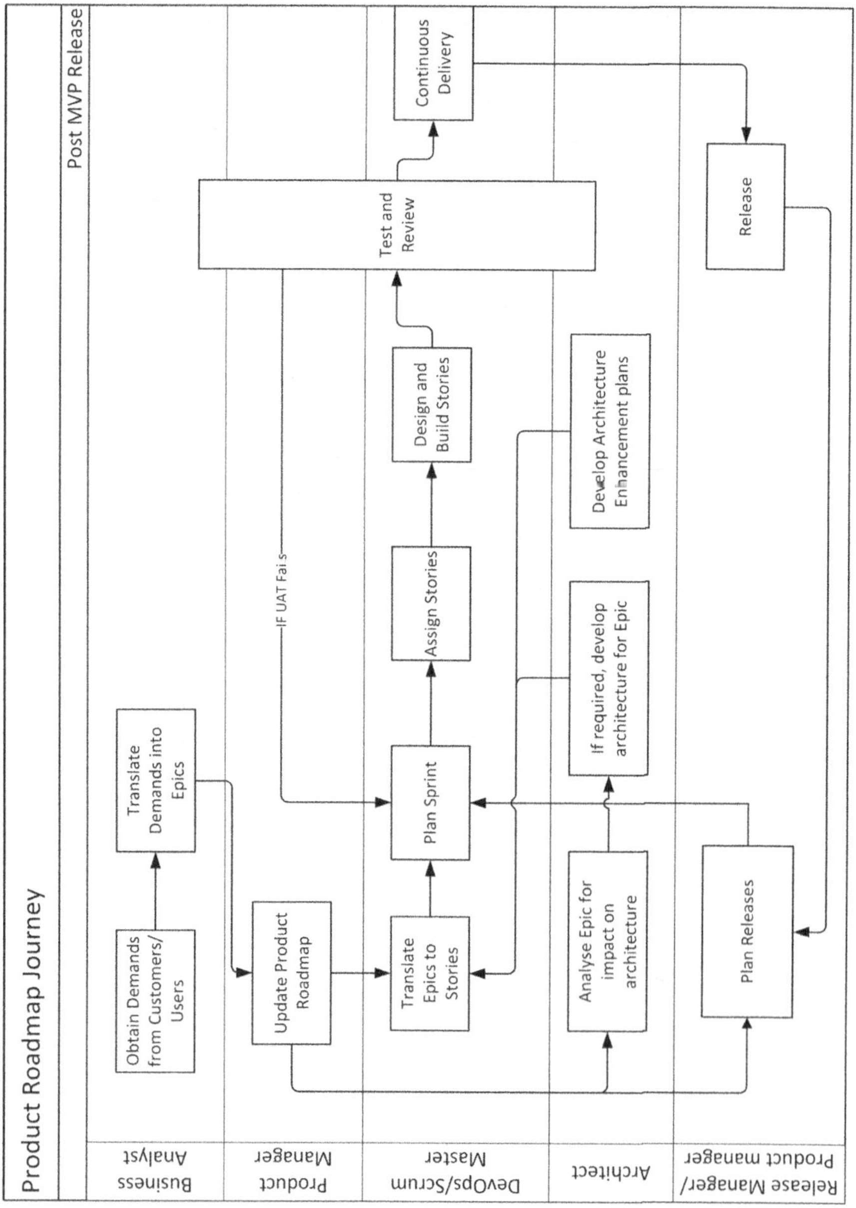

Figure 16: Ongoing Journey on product Roadmap

4.2 CI/CD

Continuous vs. continual

Continuous is among the most popular buzzword, so it is important to put forward our view on this. The general understanding is that being continuous is being without interruption while being continual has an interruption. Continuous and continual, though overlap, are not synonymous. Continual means roughly without interruption. Continuous is the thing without interruption. Continual, on the other hand, typically means 'frequently happening, with intervals between', as in the e-mail service been disrupted by continual breakdowns. ITIL books also clearly mention continual improvement as against continuous improvement. To explain with a technical analogy- continuous is analog and continual is digital. As the sampling rate increases, continual tends towards continuous. Regardless of this difference, we can continue to use both the terminologies interchangeably.

Continuous Integration

Continuous Integration is the practice that encourages developers to integrate their code into the main branch of the code repository frequently to test the code changes as soon as there is a change or commit made by a developer. It is done to ensure that the conflicts are identified and resolved as quickly as possible in the development cycle. As soon as the commit happens, the build is created, and tests are performed to validate that the change that occurred does not break the build.

As Continuous Integration captures the conflicts early, it helps to make faster releases. It is critical for teams with multiple developers as it ensures that each developer gets to check out the code, which is the most recent version to avoid conflicts.

It is a repeatable process through which the developers commit the changes multiple times. Over a while, it becomes part of the team culture that encourages iteration, feedback, and responsiveness.

Continuous Delivery

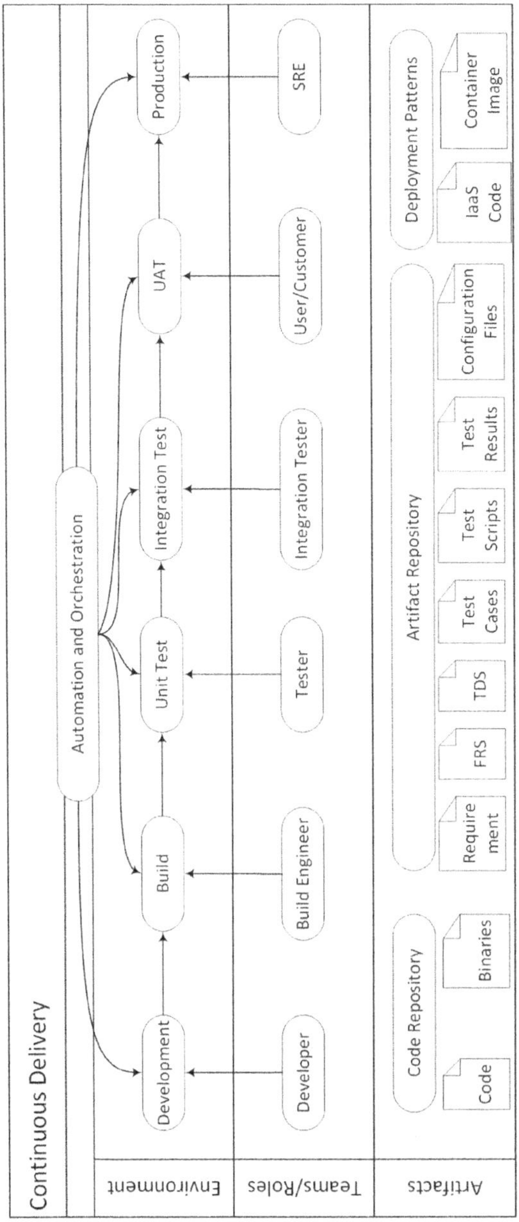

Figure 17: Continuous Delivery

Continuous Delivery is the capability to provision the environment and deploy software from one environment to another rapidly (and almost continuously). Although the industry says continuous, in reality, it is continual. Continuous Delivery capabilities are achieved by automation, which is required to accomplish an orchestration. Typical deployment involves multiple tasks in a coordinated manner, such as building and deploying binary files, setting up configurations, and applying the change configuration (if required, restart), change schema, and so on. If the software is deployed in multiple nodes, then it is even a higher degree orchestration.

It is important to note that Continuous Delivery is a must-have capability for DevOps, but Continuous Deployment is not.

Continuous Deployment

Continuous delivery is up to the development of code and releasing the code. The frequency of actually pushing into the production environment may not be right according to the DevOps sprint.

Continuous Deployment is the practice to deploy code changes in production as frequently as possible through automation. There should be no human intervention. The deployments cover everything that have passed through Continuous Integration and then through Continuous Delivery. The idea is to make frequent deployments to the customer environment so that the customers get to see the improvements more frequently. Continuous deployment seeks to deploy changes at the frequency and time different from the development time. The focus is to be able to implement whenever required though it encourages deployment at frequent intervals so that the releases are frequent with a lesser scope and are thus less surprising. It ensures that the development time can remain independent of the customer deployments. As the deployment requires pushing of features and bug fixes to customers fast, it has to be automated.

Continuous deployments are usually straightforward in terms of the ability to remain silent. However, a lot of times, the customer stakeholders need to approve before the deployment can trigger because deployment has a business impact as well as user impact.

The inputs available to a customer stakeholder to take that decision are:

1. Is it a feature release or a bug-fix release? If a bug-fix, there is no choice of whether to let the deployment happen or not.
2. Is it a pre-requisite for another release that is desired?
3. Is the currently deployed version out of support?
4. How much is the running or currently deployed version out of sync from the now released version?
5. The time it takes to upgrade to the new version
6. The complexity of upgrade to the latest version
7. Any new architectural requirements for the new version
8. Delta training needs for adopting the new version
9. Does the new version carry features that are desired?
10. Does the deployment require any manual intervention?

An interesting fact - We get updates on our mobile phones almost daily. So, continuous deployment is experienced by us daily on our mobile phone. But note that those updates are meant for our cellphone only, which is the client device, and are for the apps that are installed on our phone. The impact of the deployment is local to the device. However, for enterprise apps, the effect is far-reaching as the deployment happens on the server, which is accessed by various users. There is money charged by the application vendors at times to develop a new version and deploy it.

Sprint sizing in CI/CD

The goal is to enable continuous delivery and deployment of new features and functionality. Continuous delivery practices advocate the complete automation of the delivery pipeline — from developers committing their code to the release of the software to the user. In continuous delivery scenarios, stop points exist, allowing decision-makers to determine when to move forward. With continuous deployment, there are no stop points. Code moves directly from the time that the developers commit, through the development life cycle, to the production servers — with no human interaction whatsoever. Secure applications before they are deployed, enforcing container immutability, and quickly detecting and blocking anomalies based on the application context.

Certain products may have a more extended roadmap and continuous delivery of features/bug-fixes and enhancements managed as a product backlog. This lifecycle of the product is expected to be managed and developed by the same team who built it. However, certain other products may start in agile development methodology and continue as such for a while in their lifecycle until they move into a traditional application management methodology late in the application lifecycle as they stabilize and mature with a reduction in the number of features/enhancement requests— effectively going into a "maintenance mode." Service Providers will need to support both modes of working with the ability to perform knowledge transfer and a graceful handoff to transition support to another team or organization when required.

While the required timelines drive the sizing, the number and duration of sprints are decided upon by the DevOps team in delivering upon the features. However, it is the Product Management team that does the overall prioritization and decides upon the sprint composition. But if the product has gone into production, the clients, by providing feedback and reporting bugs, also influence the sprint composition.

Sometimes, a feature required to be built may not be deliverable within one sprint. In such cases, you could divide the features into smaller stories, and a sprint scope will then include the stories that can be delivered in a sprint. Of course, there will be little or no business value in releasing the stories built-in one sprint till the time all the stories towards the required feature have been built and delivered. Alternatively, sprint scope and duration can be changed to ensure that the complete functionality is released within one sprint.

A few such examples could be - an overhaul of the UI design of a running application, development of a sophisticated business rule engine, changes towards meeting revised performance requirements for a running application, fixing security vulnerabilities.

4.3 Container

Virtualization, as in its popular and relatively modern form, started its proliferation after 2004, though, technically LPAR form of virtualization on the mainframe existed much earlier. Virtual Windows machines were the real adoption of virtualizati on. It took more than ten years for containers to appear as the next level of virtualization. Traditional virtual machines are virtualized hardware, and containers are virtualized OS. Inside a container, one or more microservices run. A microservice is a single executable service, specially written for running as an independent application. An application would be a collection of microservices spread across one or more containers. Multiple copies of a microservice may run in various containers and linked together with load balancing and the same database for implementation. Individual containers are disposable, but there should be enough instances of a microservice running so that the overall application continues to operate. The app itself is designed to cope with individual container failure. Typical container payload is megabytes as against VM payload of gigabytes, so it does not require even minutes to provision. (it is in seconds indeed). While virtualization did not impact the application architecture, the container needs application architecture to support containerization.

Cloud Native computing is characterized by fast app delivery cycles. Containers promise this with better runtime execution and lower production infrastructure costs. Containers contain the code and the supporting libraries, binaries, and configuration files together. It helps improve the consistency and speed in deploying the applications, and reliably when moved from one environment to another. It also enhances the quality of releases as there is no customization on a delivery.

A Developer's View of making Container Choices

The container technology has been at the center of Cloud Native development. One justification of building Cloud Native applications, i.e., utilizing the power of the cloud to get your experiments to the market quickly and checking the business viability thereof justify why containers are an apt choice for hosting applications. It is backed by specific abilities that characterize the containers - quick brought-ins, scaling, dispose-offs, the security of processes, and at the same time, ease of creating and destroying. The technology provides us the advantage of achieving consistency in repeated deployments leading to improved quality in code delivery while speeding-up the pushing.

There are various container technology choices available to developers. However, there is an aspect that relates to container types in the case of having a PaaS platform in your environment, which is not brought out in the generally published material. Even though this aspect is quite fundamental and is also guided by organizational subscriptions, there is a usual problem of choice wherever developers can make a decision. Unless there is a good exposure in dealing with containers, it is difficult to understand the factors to consider. We have ourselves been at crossroads of using the relevant container type, as the choice considerations were not clear to us to start with.

First, a primer - PaaS platforms provide two choices - Buildpack-based or Platform-built and Developer-built. What are build pack-based containers - Buildpack-containers are part of the PaaS platform that is used to manage the application life cycle and are designed to run applications that get all their dependencies from build packs. Developer built containers are the containers for which the image needs to be made before it is provisioned as a container.

But then what are the considerations while deciding to host your application between the two choices. If you have the source code, you should consider using build pack-based. Advantages that it provides are developers can look for using open source runtimes rather than locking with a particular runtime, developer productivity can improve as instead of bothering to maintain images, a simple code push can automatically trigger CI/CD deployments. Applications can be deployed as source codes. A platform handles and supports the middleware and runtime to the latest versions. Images can be considered when you do not have a source code, e.g., with COTS or legacy applications or proprietary runtimes for which build packs are not available or are difficult to create. A developer has to take care of identifying middleware, runtime, and dependencies, and the developer is responsible for maintaining and managing those. We also need to note that the PaaS platforms are more opinionated about the developer-built containers. It means there could be conflicts for developers in terms of the type of access allowed. Having said this, both the choices allow similar isolation of resources through control groups, namespaces, and filesystem, and so can be considered equally secure. Both the options utilize the PaaS provided features of security, availability, failover, log streaming, and auto-scaling while trying to maintain the Cloud Native principles.

Container Technologies

There are various container technologies available. These are used to perform the management of containers, i.e., creation, administration, running, monitoring, and clustering. Container technologies are built on top of LXC (Linux Container) technology that allows running multiple containers on a single host using a single Linux kernel. The result is an environment that is close to being a standard Linux installation but without a separate kernel and has separate namespaces for users, mounts, processes, and more. LXC utilizes Linux control groups and other kernel features for assigning CPU, RAM, Disk I/O, Network I/O limits to separate processes. LXC was released in 2008, and since then, a lot of new technologies have come. Let us look at some of the most popular techniques today:

1. Docker - It is the most popular container technology from Docker Inc. to package a full application stack. Docker gives a standard way to build container images using the Dockerfile. Docker also provides the container runtime. Docker image format has become a de facto standard with the popularity of Docker.
2. Rocket - Another container runtime, it is from CoreOS. It follows an image format, ACI, which is different from Docker.
3. Cloud Foundry - It is the platform to manage Cloud Foundry as well as Docker containers and is supported by Cloud Foundry Foundation.
4. Kubernetes - It is the platform that originated from Google in 2014 and is used to manage the Docker and rkt containers.
5. Red Hat's Open Shift Container Platform - It is an on-premises platform as a service having a core of application containers that are powered by Docker. Kubernetes provide the orchestration and management of these containers. The platform runs on a foundation of Red Hat Enterprise Linux.

Docker Swarm is the platform built by Docker Inc. to orchestrate docker based containers. Both Kubernetes and Docker Swarm are used to deploy containers inside a cluster. However, Kubernetes has taken over the industry and has become a de-facto standard technology for Docker container management.

Cloud Foundry vs. Kubernetes

- Both use containers to host your application. Cloud Foundry can run both Docker and Garden containers. For Garden containers, Cloud Foundry uses the Diego system for container management.
- Both offer the flexibility to run in hybrid/multi-cloud environments, allowing you to choose among different cloud

providers and, if required, split the workload between on-premise and public cloud.

- Both technologies support the ability to deploy applications with zero downtime, Kubernetes has a superior built-in mechanism for zero-downtime deployments with rollback.
- Both provide container management features such as deployment, scaling, load balancing, logging, and monitoring.

But Cloud Foundry is a PaaS platform, whereas Kubernetes is not a typical PaaS system. Therefore, the differences lie in the ease of use by the developer's vs. portability achieved through container management.

Cloud Foundry	Kubernetes
Developers can develop their applications on the local machines, run and test them on local servers and push the applications to the cloud. Cloud Foundry picks the right buildpack, and a lot of the configuration is done automatically.	Developers will build the image locally and push it to an image repository. Kubernetes uses the image in the repository to provision containers.
Limits the types of applications to the ones whose runtimes and buildpacks are supported.	It does not constraint the support for different application types. All it requires is the container image that has the binaries and the dependencies together.

Provides services to deploy source code and build an application using the CI/CD mechanism.	Build and deployment of the application are through application image.
Provides application - level additional services like middleware, databases, etc. used to build the application features.	It does not provide application-level services.
Developer convenience approach *"Here's my code. Run it on the cloud for me. I don't care how."*	SRE convenience approach *"Here's my code. I will tell you exactly how you should run it on the cloud for me."*
Supports route-based load balancing in the traditional server-side configuration inside the cluster as well as client-side load balancing by using native platform features.	Uses DNS-based resolution to identify other services within the cluster. The primary benefit that Kubernetes' load balancing offers is not requiring any special client libraries.
The fundamental principle of a cloud foundry application is entire statelessness. It follows the 12-factor	Kubernetes can attach a storage volume to your container, and you can attach a storage volume to any of your containers.

apps model, and one of these models assumes that your application has no state. Any storage-based requirement is fulfilled through either a platform service or a storage service outside the cloud foundry cluster itself. It is an advantage or a disadvantage depending on your application and architecture. However, for stateless applications, it is always a good idea not to use any internal storage.	It means you get a reliable storage solution, which lets you run storage-based containers like a database or a file server.
Developers can focus only on the development	More work for developers to build and maintain the images.
The main advantage is the ease of use	The main advantage is portability

4.4 Microservice

Microservice is an intricate pattern in the Cloud Native app world that is the solution to many problems but also the cause of the problem to the network world.

Microservices architecture has caught the fancy of software developers and architects and is now being seen as more and more appealing for modern application development. Even though inter-process communication is not a new thing, the popularity of the architecture since it came in the reckoning in 2011 has got pronounced in the last two years with cloud-native application development picking up pace. Microservices architecture and its benefits are fairly well known. However, architects have been under a dilemma of when to implement it (or rather when not) in an application's development journey. We are putting forth our views on this through this article in a bid to help architects decide.

Pre-requisites

Teams working on new applications these days have a standard charter - build a cloud-native application, to be able to utilize cloud features as well as for faster turnaround. Building a Cloud Native application does not necessarily mean starting with microservices itself. Saying that all Cloud Native applications follow the microservice architecture is a misnomer.

Monoliths can also be Cloud Native by following the Twelve-factor principle. Our recommendation is to consider building monolith in the absence of all the prerequisites and, at the same time, develop a modular approach for development. However, one needs to take care that each component has well-defined boundaries and a clear scope of what it does or does not need to do. It will help when one refactors the application later to adopt the architecture. We will go a step-ahead and recommend always start building with a monolith, and when you are ready to take, refactor the existing components into microservices and design the new functionalities as microservices. Microservices architecture requires specific prerequisites that need to be in place before it can be adopted.

1. Prerequisite 1 - Application to be modeled based on the business domain it is a part of.
2. Prerequisite 2 – The components should be highly mutable.
3. Prerequisite 3 – Team structured as per the application model.
4. Prerequisite 4 - Support for multiple databases in your application.
5. Prerequisite 5 – Database consistency model in BaSE form.
6. Prerequisite 6 – The team has skills in adding and maintaining ReST and messaging-based communication layers.

More about these pre-requisites have been covered in a later section in this book.

Essentials for Running

We will also mention here a few things that need attention for running the microservice-based implementations.

1. Setup a choreography of microservices - Client-side load balancing, registry, discovery, and circuit breaker patterns are required.
2. Consider using a gateway to avoid direct chats to avoid coding and refactoring complexities as well as to ensure protocol compatibilities.
3. Your testing strategy should be comprehensive - Unit, Integration, Contract, End-to-end, and Performance.
4. Only take what is required as a client – Take nothing more than what you need to minimize risks associated with later changes in definition.
5. Keep an eye on latency that you introduce with microservices. Abort the microservice if the functionality is

performance-critical, hugely transactional across application boundaries, and any lag added because communication across boundaries will not be acceptable to the business.

6. Be mindful of the fact that you cannot have services defined right always, and you may have to change your service definitions a lot of times before you could finally have well-defined services with zero or minimal overlap.
7. Depending on the perceived frequency of changes, business capability(s) being tried to address, clarity in the definition of interfaces, and dependencies and overlaps in functionality and data being stored, you may also have to merge two services into one.

Without the prerequisites being met, please do not implement microservices architecture for the sake of having a Cloud Native application as it will lead you to more significant problems. Architects need to give a serious thought on their readiness before venturing into the world of microservices.

4.4.1 IP Network constraints for Microservices

Networks were built for a purpose with different protocols. IBM SNA, Xerox XNS, Digital DECnet (and LAT), Banyan Vines, Novel Netware IPX/SPX. Novel Netware ruled the position of Network Operation System for PC for several years in the early 90s. And then finally, TCP/IP emerged as the winner.

So, if we have to build the network today, it would not be what we see today. It is built on the OSI seven-layer model, and probably the need for the 8th layer is now emerging because, in the new world, developers are looking more from the traditional IP networks.

What IP Network can deliver is the availability, speed, security, and reliability of data communication. But data has a context in the modern world, and additional considerations for that expose some of the constraints of traditional IP networks, and a few are discussed here.

TCP Flow controls are not good enough

For most applications of TCP/IP, the TCP controls are sufficient to ensure that the data is transmitted at a rate optimal to avoid swamping the receiver end or the links along the path. Congestion control prevents congesting the path from the sender to the receiver, and the receive window ensures that the receiver is not overwhelmed with data more than it can handle. However, in most modern applications, excessive data and media stream transmission, are increasingly becoming business as usual. TCP flow controls were not designed for such scenarios. If desired, the application can provide additional flow control if it is not required for the application data to transmit to the client as fast as TCP would allow. The application may limit the data transmission rate. The TCP control mechanisms would still apply. So application flow control effects are reduced if the TCP controls already limit the connection.

One of the most common examples of effective application-level flow control is implemented in YouTube to conserve bandwidth and prevent the client connection from being saturated. YouTube is among the most popular website on the Internet and a significant contributor to the HTTP traffic and demonstrated the augmentation of flow control on top of TCP flow control.

Where is the protection of partitioning?

All business-critical applications run on the cluster. A cluster can split into separate running systems when members lose the ability to see each other. The typical cause of this problem is a failure in the network. It is referred to as the network partitioning and synonym with the network failure in the cluster world. When a partitioned system is detected, only one side of the system keeps running, and the other side automatically shuts down.

While the TCP connection ping is used to detect failed members in the cluster. TCP keepalives are an optional feature in TCP/IP stack, and the keepalive packet contains no data, and it is used for connection keep-alive purposes.

At the infrastructure level, a public cloud service provider can offer a private cloud that is a dedicated, specially secured partition of the public cloud. Network partitioning ensures that the private cloud is virtually isolated from other resources in the public cloud. The virtual private cloud can also be integrated into the enterprise data center using an encrypted communication link, such as a virtual private network (VPN) connection.

At the data layer, data stores can be distributed across various network partitions to protect the access to data, thus ensuring high availability and segregation of the data between multiple entities logically. However, data replication to synchronize data between various partitions is required to be considered.

At the application level, the network of the containers creates an isolated environment for container instances that run in the space allocated to the enterprise. Containers that are connected to the same network are assigned a private IP address based on the default network settings. To make a container available to the public, there is a need to expose a public port and bind a public IP address to the container. One can replace the default network settings and create an own private overlay network with a custom IP address range. Each application is isolated and runs in its container or virtual machine. Security groups can be configured to isolate each container or virtual machine.

Session-based routing against packet-based routing

Session-based routing is an application-centric design that routes entire sessions instead of routing individual packets. A TCP session is a series of interactions between two communication endpoints that occur during a connection's lifespan.

Legacy internet routers and protocols work on individual packets and IP addresses and not on sessions. Session-based routing operates on the entire communication exchange being a bidirectional flow and sessions being managed at each router. As cloud, mobility, and security concepts continue to be popular among trends; network architecture is also becoming dynamic to address session-based routing an effective solution.

Cloud service providers are responsible for maintaining networks connecting the cloud resources. Cloud provider ensures the accessibility of the network services. The provider also is responsible for the protection and monitoring of the internal networks and the connections between customer and cloud services.

In packet routing, the network packet's application layer data is not scrutinized and does not track the state of connections. Packet routing has minimal scrutiny for access through the firewall. If the rule check passes, the packet is allowed to be routed through the firewall as per the rules in the routing table. However, in session routing, an application-level firewall evaluates network packets for valid data at the application layer before allowing a connection and maintains complete connection state and sequencing information. The firewall can validate other security items such as user password and service requests that appear in the application layer data. Proxy services manage traffic through firewalls for a specific service such as HTTP or FTP. Proxy services can provide increased access control to allow access to some while denying access to others, hide internal IP addresses, conduct detailed checks for valid data, as well as generate audit records about the traffic transferred. Proxy, based on configuration, may also perform functions such as URL filtering, modification of data, logging of authentication, and caching of HTTP objects.

The packet-based routing which works on Layer 3 is no more suitable for cloud-based applications as there are thousands of applications hosted on a single cloud masked by multiple IP addresses. To support session-based routing that works on Layer 7, the router technology has got significantly enhanced, and these routers now do a more in-depth inspection of traffic to identify the target.

Session routing in the cloud is applied through routers that provide comprehensive WAN gateway and network services. These routers can provide dynamic routing of the traffic across the best link based on up to minute application performance, bandwidth usage, data privacy, and availability of WAN links. The deployed routers can monitor, control, move, and report on streams of application data. These can-do deep packet inspections and identify and control thousands of applications.

4.4.2 Augmentation over IP networks for Microservices

IP network does not deliver all the requirements of today's Cloud Native app world, and despite adding new products like

HTTP/2 and gRPC, the gap is still huge. Hence, we require augmentation, primarily because multiple microservices in the system present newer challenges in maintaining the communication also because of the transient nature of the application's estate in the cloud. Microservices form distributed systems, and instead of just a method call away, network calls need to be made to consume them. Therefore, it is essential to wire them to allow the microservices within a composed system to communicate with each other. Primary requirements that need to be fulfilled by augmentation are:

Location Finding - How does a microservices locate each other? One way is to hard-code the address in the code or a configuration file. However, what if the address keeps changing because of transiency, which leads to locations changing with time.

Service Discovery can address this. The client service searches a service based on its name and metadata in the Service Registry, and the reference obtained contains a direct link to a microservice to be used. Service discovery allows microservices to be registered and consumers to look for services, and also provide information about the registrations and de-registrations of services. It is upon a microservice to de-register itself once it is out of operation. The Service Registry is a listing of all services and makes them available to other services through a client library. Each microservice needs to register itself in the registry. It is possible by applying either server-side or client-side discovery tools.

In the case of server-side discovery, a router, proxy, a load balancer, or an API Gateway is used to discover a service. The client gets a virtual address.

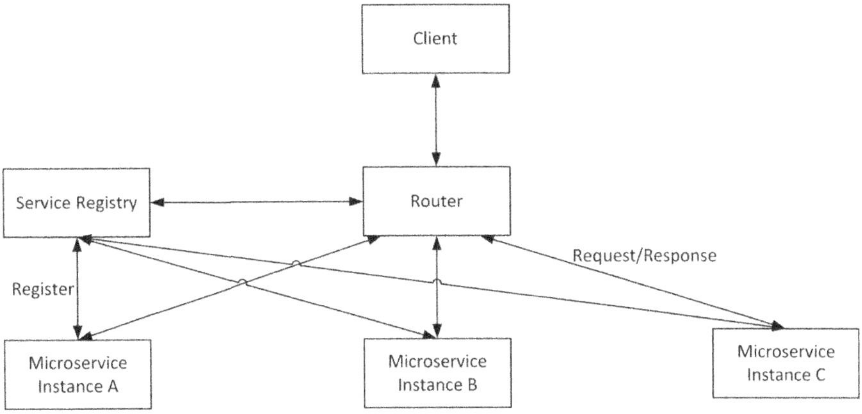

Figure 18: Server side Service Discovery

Having these externally or as a centralized solution like is not advisable as it may prove to be a throughout infrastructure failure.

In case of client-side discovery, the client itself looks upon the registry for the address and then invokes the backend service. It can also perform load balancing. Routing and load balancing is the responsibility of the client.

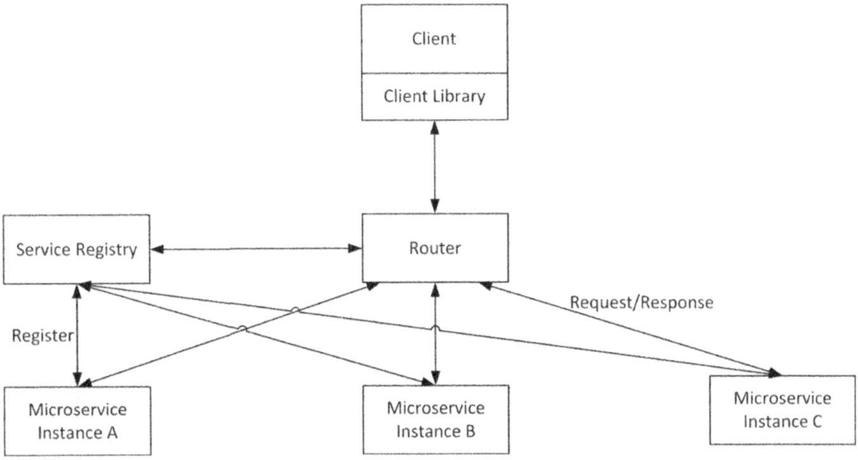

Figure 19: Client side Service Discovery

For Service Discovery, we used Netflix OSS software - Eureka as the Service Registry and Ribbon as the Http Service Client in our product. The client-side discovery was implemented using various Spring Cloud annotations.

Example:

```
@Configuration
@EnableEurekaClient
@Profile(Array("enableEureka"))
class EurekaClientConfiguration {
 @Bean
 @LoadBalanced
  def restTemplate(scalaObjectMapper : ScalaObjectMapper) :
RestTemplate = {
   val restTemplate = new RestTemplate()
   restTemplate.getMessageConverters foreach {
    case mc: MappingJackson2HttpMessageConverter =>
     mc.setObjectMapper(scalaObjectMapper)
    case _ =>
   }
   restTemplate
 }
```

The @EnableEurekaClient annotation enables the Eureka client. The @LoadBalanced annotation configures the RestTemplate to use Ribbon, which has been set to use the Eureka client to make service discovery. As a result, the RestTemplate will handle requests to the endpoint by querying Eureka to find the network locations of available service instances.

Load Balancing – How do we load balance between multiple instances of a microservice? How do we timeout a service call? Can it be only interval-based or can also be after a defined number of retries?

It can be addressed by the Load Balancer either centrally or as part of the Service Client library implemented for Service Discovery. Load balancing can be achieved through various algorithms like round-robin, average response-time weighted, random, or service availability.

Fault Avoidance - Microservices based applications have more potential failure points as each call may traverse one or more microservices.

These configurations are possible to do through circuit breakers. Circuit breakers prevent calling a failed service again and again. If a microservice fails or the timeout, circuit breaker checks if the failure count has exceeded a threshold. In case it is so, the circuit breaker switches to an open state from the closed state. In an open state, calls to the circuit breaker will start failing, and the circuit breaker will execute a fallback. After a pre-defined amount of time, the circuit breaker gets in a half-opened state to try the service call again. Upon the outcome of this call, the circuit breaker will reset and may wither return to the closed state until another timeout elapses, or to the open state.

We implemented Hystrix, which is another Netflix OSS software as the circuit breaker technology in ServiceXchange. It is unique from many other circuit breaker implementations in that it operates each circuit breaker within its thread pool and collects metrics like status, traffic volume, request rate, error percentage, hosts reporting, latency percentiles, successes, failures, and rejections.

```
@SpringBootApplication
@EnableCircuitBreaker
public class Application {
```

```
    public static void main(String[] args) {
        new SpringApplicationBuilder(Application.-
class).web(true).run(args);
    }

}

@Component
public class ShoppingCatalog {

    @HystrixCommand(fallbackMethod = "defaultCatalog")
    public Object getCatalog(Map<String, Object> parameters) {
        //functionality
    }

    public Object defaultCatalog (Map<String, Object> parame-
ters) {
        return catalog;
    }
}
```

Health checks - How to detect if a microservice is unavailable? How do we know if a service has crashed?

Each microservice provides an API that responds with the health of the service. If it is found unhealthy, it should not be called anymore, and fail-over can be invoked.

We implemented a Spring Boot Actuator to implement health checks in ServiceXchange microservices. We also implemented custom health indicators.

```
@Component
```

```
public class CheckHealth implements HealthIndicator {

  @Override
  public Health health() {
    int nmerror = check(); // perform some specific health check
    if (nmerror != 0) {
      return Health.down()
       .withDetail("Error Code", nmerror).build();
    }
    return Health.up().build();
  }

  public int check() {
    /* checked the health here */
    return 0;
  }
}
```

API Gateway - Can a single-entry point be implemented? API gateways provide a single entry point to all microservices. They can transform requests and can also translate protocols to communicate with a target microservice.

4.4.3 Service Mesh: The right augmentation for CN world

Typical overheads in direct communication between microservice to microservice include discovering a service, opening of a TCP port, establish a connection with another service, establish flow control, implement security for data transfer, and so on. And when there are a large number of microservices and each of them dealing with the same overheads, the amount adds up significantly. One efficient and effective method is to add a small proxy alongside each microservice. The proxy is deployed into a process or container that is separate from the application process or container. It provides isolation and encapsulation from the application. The proxy is a supporting feature for every microservice, and the separate processor container that deploys a supporting component is called as a sidecar. Service mesh also brings in a control plane to manage all the sidecars in the ecosystem. The service mesh is thus a "mesh" system of control plane and sidecars.

What is the need?

Service mesh optimizes the inter-service communication by routing requests from one service to another. But do microservices not communicate freely already without the service mesh? Yes, the microservices do communicate already, as depicted below, through a lightweight communication protocol.

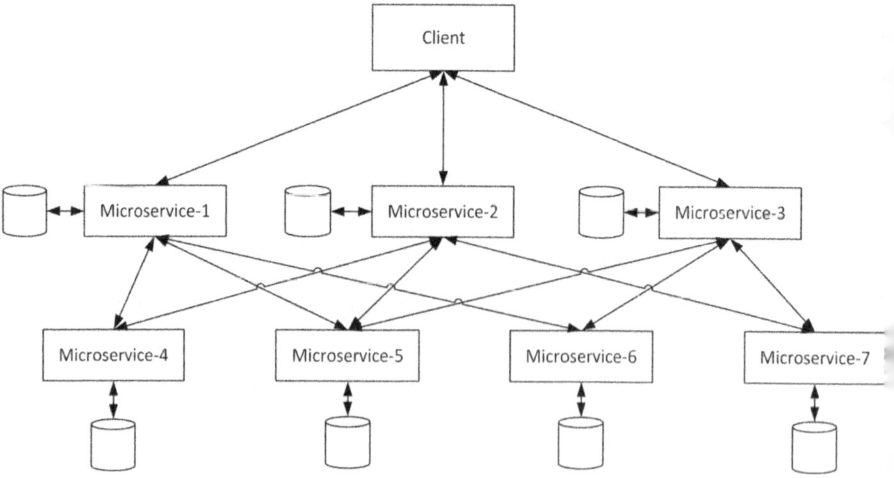

Figure 20: Service to Service Communication Complexity

But when the number of services grows, and the number of service instances in an application instance grows, the number of endpoints grows with the frequency of changes resulting in complicating network communications. The service mesh addresses this complexity by doing traffic management, thus optimizing communication. Service mesh takes the logic of service to service communication away from the service code to another layer. This layer contains an array of proxies, one proxy for each app, and the communication between two microservices is through the attached proxies rather than directly.

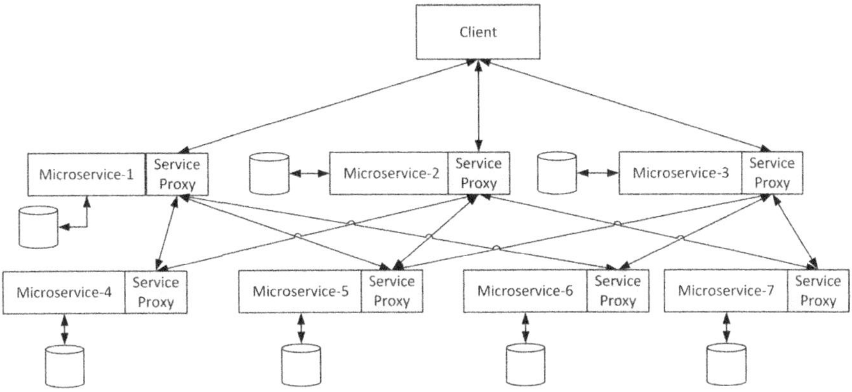

Figure 21: Service to Service Communication Simplified with Mesh

The purpose of a proxy is to route or proxy the traffic to and from the container it is attached to. The proxy network is managed through an orchestration framework, which consists of a Control Plane and a Data Plane. The Data Plane manages the network traffic to and from microservices through the associated proxies. The Control Pane generates and deploys the configuration that controls the behavior of the Data Plane and can be used to observe and trace the behavior of microservice communications. There are rules configured for communications, and over a while, these rules can be tweaked for further optimizing the communications, e.g., changing the retrial time, the number of retries, etc.

The traffic from external sources, e.g., the UI application to a microservice, is termed north-south traffic while from microservice to microservice, is termed as east-west traffic.

Other Advantages

Service mesh proxies can provide you with a bunch of other functionalities like load balancing, circuit breaking, service discovery, encryption, authentication, and monitoring. In a microservice architecture, the mixture of business functionalities and these additional configurations require a tight coupling, which increases the overall application complexity since the developer now needs also to understand how these components are configured to be able to troubleshoot in case of any issues. Hence from an application standpoint, service mesh lets application contain just the implementation of business functionalities rather than also implementing the logic to communicate with other services.

Let us look at these advantages in little more detail here.

1. Discovery - Services discovered automatically between data plane and control plane wither through DNS lookup or automatic registration with the service registry.

2. Load balancing - This could be done based on service versions or algorithms like a round-robin or least load basis or also on a blue-green or canary deployment basis facilitated by layer 7 load balancing capabilities.

3. Fault Tolerance - Timeouts and retrials can be built into the rule configurations, including circuit breaking and error injection. Timeout intervals and the maximum number of retries before an error is incurred can be configured as rules in the control plane. There is a built-in circuit breaker. Fault

can also be injected selectively to test resiliency without affecting all users.

4. Security - Each service to service communication is secure, authenticated, and authorized. Each communication is logged for access and privilege. Ingress access can be validated through various authentication mechanisms, including SSO solutions with MFA.

5. Encryption - Messages between microservices are encrypted through TLS/mTLS and generally include a certificate manager.

6. Policy and Telemetry - Service mesh also provides a flexible way to enforce authorization policies and be able to collect telemetry for the services. An example of a policy could be setting the quota limit, which could be either done at the sidecar level or ingress/egress level.

7. Monitoring - Real-time monitoring is possible, based on telemetry. Built-in analytics ensure a view of telemetric data on performance, security, and traffic volume along with visualization of service connections and traffic tracing.

4.5 Degree of Cloud Nativity

It is not essential to adhere to all twelve factors to become Cloud Native. An application can be Cloud Native without having a microservice architecture. The diagram below depicts the degree of cloud nativity that is achieved by following various levels of the twelve factors.

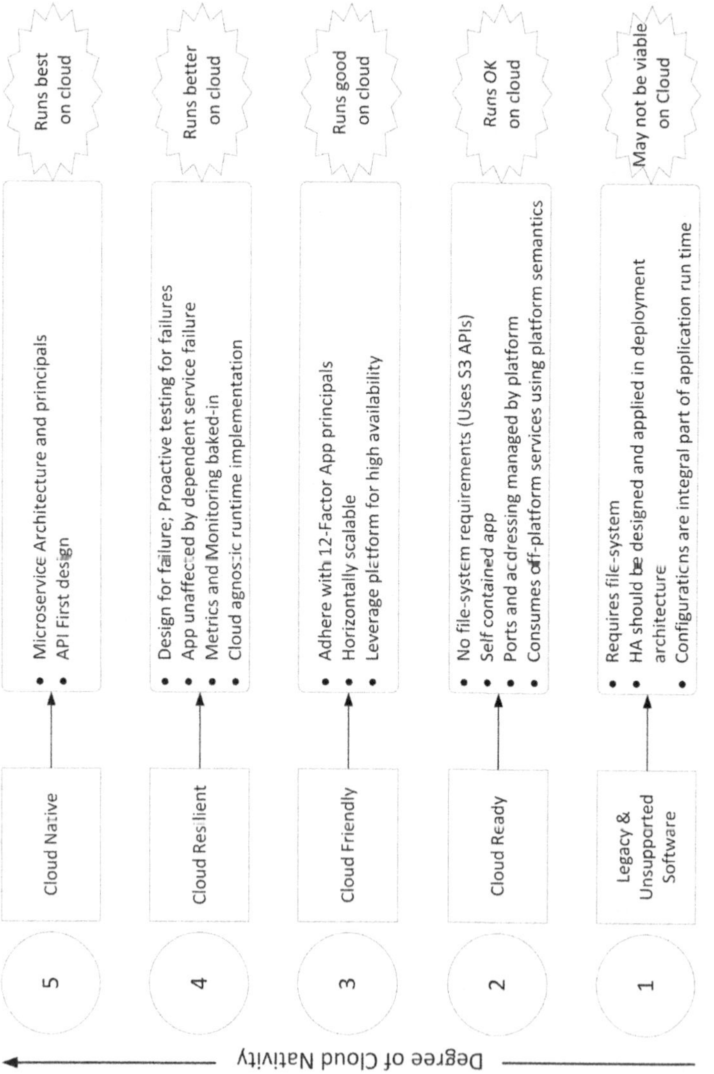

Figure 22: Degree of Cloud Nativity

Cloud Readiness

Cloud Readiness is the stage at which we determine if an application is an appropriate candidate to be modernized and made Cloud Native. Some of the criteria are:

a. How tightly coupled are the application services
b. Infrastructure dependency (Network/Storage)
c. Data coupling - does data need to be consolidated and stored locally?
d. Does the application rely on OS-specific features?

Cloud friendliness

- Cloud Friendliness is the point where we understand an application's adherence to the Twelve-factor application design approach. In the initial stages of creating a roadmap for Cloud Friendliness, we determine the minimum number of the twelve factors that must be met before applications can run in the cloud.
- In this stage, we also assess the application ability to scale horizontally and leveraging the platform's high availability.

Cloud resilience

- Cloud Resilience ensures the application is designed for and proactively tested for failure. Cloud resiliency can be built into the PaaS specific platform itself. It can also refer to IT resources being redundant within the same cloud but in different locations or across clouds. Application reliability and availability can increase by leveraging the resiliency of cloud-based IT resources.
- In this scenario, applications designed to run on any cloud implementation and are not affected by dependent service failures. They may also have built-in monitoring and metrics.

Cloud Native

- As we get to the highest level of maturity in the Cloud Native Maturity Model, we ensure that applications adhere to a

Microservice Architecture and Principles and follow an API-first design strategy.

- We ensure that we are taking advantage of all aspects of a Cloud Native based delivery model.
- Utilizing a DevOps approach
- Conforming to a Continuous Integration/Continuous Delivery strategy
- Fully utilizing Microservices
- Implementing a container-based approach to microservices

4.6 Migration to Cloud

The adoption of the cloud has been on the rise. Enterprises have realized the need for migration of application estate from on-premises to cloud. However, the movement of an existing application from the data center to the cloud is not a straight forward lift and shift. It presents lots of challenges, and there are chances that an application has to be dropped from the "to-be migrated" list simply because it is massively entangled to its existing ecosystem and carries little business justification to put in the amount of effort required. For this purpose, an assessment is critical to identify the candidates for migration. Generally, it is a phased approach and uses various strategies that vary in terms of effort and time taken to migrate. The assessment and migration exercises are specialized jobs mystifying the architects with choices which they need to evaluate in line with their organization's requirements. Of course, each architect has to consider the availability of IT skills and the amount of budget in the enterprise, apart from the enterprise's architecture principles.

As mentioned before, the architects have various choices to make in terms of evaluating the migration strategies and the supporting services available from service providers. For an application, if the assessment has proven that the ROI to migrate is justified, the approach to migrate could range from simply changing the application hosts from in-premise to on-cloud or could require an altogether re-writing the application to be on the cloud. Here's a sneak preview of strategies along with the value it gives. One needs to choose the right approach for each application, which is a candidate for migration.

1. Retain - Strategy is to choose to retain the application as-is. Used as a strategy where the application is unsupported or is about to sunset, and there is no business justification to move to a cloud.
2. Retire - Strategy is that the application is not required any more since there are other applications already on the cloud that provide this application's functionalities. The strategy is to retire or decommission this application completely.
3. Rehost - Strategy is to change the app configuration to re-deploy on the cloud. It is mostly used for packaged apps which do not have an active roadmap and have ad-hoc environments. There is no change in code except any code required for the changing of hosts.
4. Replatform - Strategy is to upgrade the application platform, e.g., the OS or DB. The objective is to start using cloud services rather than on-premise. Suitable for applications that do not need to be fully Cloud Native. There is no change in code except any code required for changing to use the cloud services.
5. Refactor - Developers continue to use the languages and frameworks they know but recode to break the application into components to start using continuous integration/continuous deployment.
6. Rebuild - Strategy is to discard what is written and start from scratch simply because the existing code is too intricate or is poorly designed that even refactoring is going to be a failure.

Despite the complexity, time requirements, and total costs of this type of project, rebuilding proves worthwhile for applications when refactoring is not feasible.

7. Replace - End using the existing app and start using third party software, which is delivered as a service.

Migrating to the cloud requires the adoption of Cloud Native architecture. But why? It is because of the various advantages it provides. Let us look at some of these now.

1. Quicker Builds - Cloud Native means quicker builds and quicker deliveries, and the applications can run as always-on, elastic-scale services.
2. Flexibility - Applications that run on one cloud can run on any cloud without modification.
3. Developer motivation - Developers are saved from the overhead of writing code to run and scale across cloud infrastructures. So, they can focus on writing code that delivers customer value.
4. Lean operations - Leaner operations team that focuses on process improvement in place of routine admin tasks as patching and upgrades at all levels of the stack are automated, thus removing the need for a team with admin expertise.

4.7 Cloud Native does not necessarily mean robust

The robustness of an application refers to the ability to withstand the adverse use cases. Robustness of code deals with all the things that shouldn't happen but inevitably do. In contrast, happy path programming only deals with correctness under perfect conditions. The correctness bugs in happy path programming are logical flaws and produce unacceptable results, while robustness bugs stop perfectly-good logic from working.

A Cloud Native application designed to run on the cloud does not automatically make the codes robust. Typically, business application software is buggy and fragile (not sturdy) mostly because usually programs are too big and too complicated for a single developer to comprehend completely, and thus it is difficult for developers to be able to discover and eliminate all the errors or even to be confident as to what extent of errors exist. It is especially true concerning subtle errors that only make their presence known in unusual circumstances. The microservices architecture breaks the large programs into smaller pieces and eliminates one of the (primary) factors that contribute to the fragility of the application program.

Robustness should be designed into software from the ground up and cannot be successfully tackled later. The lack of planning for robustness is a significant factor in the numerous security and stability. However, quality assurance helps to detect the fragility of the software. The flaky test manifests the weakness of software. A flaky test is a quality assurance (QA) test that fails to produce consistent results. Ideally, each time the code is tested, the results are consistent. The system will either work as expected and pass the test or not work as expected and fail the test. Sometimes, however, QA tests on the same code, using the same configurations, will produce inconsistent results. When this happens, the test is labeled "flaky". It is a direct indication of robustness failure. If you are aiming at robustness, then it is the point to halt the development of the application, thoroughly investigate the cause of the flaky test, and resolve it. If left unresolved and there truly is an issue with the code, one problem has the potential to wind up leading to another and another as more are built onto the incorrect code.

4.7.1 Best Practices for Robust Application

Robustness of Product vs. Robustness of Solution

A solution may consist of one or more products. A defect in a product will result in a defective solution. However, a defective product is not the only probable reason for an imperfect solution. The framework created out of multiple products may be broken because of the incompatibility of products that may, in turn, cause the solution to be defective. The other reason could be the design of the solution and not the product itself. We talk about the robustness of the product here and not the solution.

Product Robustness

In my first publication, I have discussed the robust process design. Application codes are a kind of codification of specific processes; therefore, the generic principles will be similar, but, in this section, we want to confine to the application design and code perspective solely.

Well designed: Thorough design with every detail, exhaustive documentation, no spec left to the guesswork of developer

Neat and tidy: Neat pieces of code are easily readable and use proper name conventions.

Well named: good, consistent and solid naming convention

Well tested: Testing for an application ensures that its functionality and usability are tested. Testing helps to enhance the quality of the software and, at the same time, identify in advance the adverse situations that can impact the robustness. Testing is carried out both manually and in an automated way through scripts. There are various frameworks available for automation. Testing needs to cover the following aspects of an application with the motive of finding situations in which the application becomes unstable or incapable of executing:

1. Functional - Test the desired functionality with specific inputs and check for the desired outputs. Commonly used frameworks and tools are Selenium, HP QTP, IBM Rational Functional Testing tool.
2. Performance - Test whether the application performs well under the desired load. You can use third-party tools to simulate the desired loads.
3. Cross-browser - Whether the application works on desired browsers.
4. Security - Testing for security vulnerabilities in the application. Tools for static testing try to find vulnerabilities in the source code and ensures to some extent that the coding standards are adhered to without executing the code. Tools for dynamic testing try to find vulnerabilities in a running application. Interactive testing combines elements of both static and dynamic testing by placing an agent inside the app. Tools for interactive tests cover more code, produce more accurate results, and verify a broader range of security rules. Tools for Runtime Application Self Protection try to protect the application from malicious input or behavior by using the app to monitor its action, and in the case so, it alerts and optionally blocks the execution.

4.7.2 The general guidance for robustness

Eliminate the need to check return values. Use exceptions when normal flow cannot continue. Stop using true, false, and NULL as error responses. Return NULL only when "no data" is a valid response. Throw an exception when "no data" is not a correct response.

Type mismatches break perfectly sound logic. Check incoming data before using it. For example, Type-hinting only tells you if something is the right shape. Type-hinting does not validate your data. Checks and Requirements can help. Unsupported outputs can break logic. An incompatible state can also break logic. Unhandled errors and uncaught exceptions, ultimately crash the code.

1. Check everything before you use it.
2. Check both types and conditions.
3. Don't propagate bad data.

At times, checks on input data for matching patterns may be required. For example, a phone number value input by the user should follow a particular pattern. Another example could be an email address.

Other checks could be on a range of values. For example, the quantity ordered for an item can only be in the range of 1-10.

For building robustness of the application, the emphasis is to try to handle all expected situations with the data, which may impact the application functioning as well as availability. However, the other aspect of robustness is to build fault tolerance in the application, which means that in case of unexpected inputs, i.e., the ones which are not handled, the application should still gracefully handle such data.

4.7.3 Robustness of code vs. robustness of operations

The robustness of a product is also manifested through the effectiveness and efficiency of the operations associated with it. Smooth operations are dependent upon the following aspects of code:

1. Code should be robust
2. Code should look at the configuration parameters to let the application switch between various cloud services
3. A golden instance of the application is always available that carries the most recent version of each codebase for any reference.
4. The code should be automatically deployable.
5. The code should allow both horizontal and vertical scalability.

Even though the code maintenance is not a part of operations, it is a good idea to follow best practices on source code which will help the code maintenance and indirectly improve or maintain the robustness of code. For example:

1. Comments can be added anywhere, which the developer thinks that will help other developers to understand the pieces of code. From an operations point of view, commenting the code around setting up connections to services is essential to allow operations to change the connections fast in case there is a change in service endpoints. Ideally, the connection parameters should be a part of the configuration of the application, but in case not, comments are handy for the Operations to change the services being used quickly.

2. Hooks for debugging - Log statements help trace the flow of control in a program and thus help isolate the issue or potential areas of the cause. While setting up log messages, the severity of the message can be set up by the developer. The level of logging should vary as per the environment in which the code is running to filter out the log levels which are not required to be traced in that environment. The levels should be configurable and made to change as per the environment.

4.7.4 Robust programming in the DevOps model

In the DevOps model, QA is aligned in the DevOps cycle. Testing engineers have to ensure that the test cases are 100% covered and help identify the failures. It requires the test environments are standardized. All the testing tasks should be aligned with the Continuous Integration cycle. The test cases, along with the exit criteria needed to be executed for a particular build, need to be identified and for which test engineers and developers need to collaborate. Test engineers should execute the related test cases to achieve 100% code coverage. The cycle of testing and bug fixing should be iteratively run till the code becomes stable enough to be released.

Robust programming in the DevOps model continues to implement the handlers for all data elements related to any new functionality or feature being implemented. It also seeks to identify and meet and new failures. However, certain types of failures, to be handled, require design changes in the application. It could result in either modifying the design itself or settling for a compromise.

Robust programming is a way to achieve robustness of the application, and building robustness in the app is a continual exercise that is taken up to meet failures identified as unhandled. Some measures can be deployed early in the design. However, there are new failures that get identified over a while and thus need to be handled later in the design. Though late changes are costlier, the inevitability of encountering a failure lately cannot be ruled out.

4.7.5 *Jugaad* culture and robustness

Jugaad is an innovative fix or a work-around, that often either bends a rule, or can be used in a way to turn a rule. It is also often used to signify creativity: to make existing things work or to create new things with meager resources. *Jugaad* can be a strength in product operation but a weakness in product development. If an organization's value system is designed for *Jugaad*, then the product will never be robust.

***Jugaad* is innovation but not sustainable:** *Jugaad* may be a strength for the application run, but it is a weakness in product build to run across multiple customers.

***Jugaad* is agile but not sustainable-** because quickness is the essence of the *jugaad*, not sustainability.

Temptation for *Jugaad*

Since it is meant to deliver a solution with meager resources, the essence is to provide a fix in the least amount of time. In the zest to be immediate, the delivery of solutions in the most righteous way gets compromised most of the time in such situations. It may be helpful if it is in response to a bug or a crisis but spells doom for the application in the long run. It is because the fix can:

1. run contrary to some other existing feature.
2. require more such fixes to meet another requirement.
3. lead to a deadlock when there is a competing requirement.
4. lead to performance problems when such fixes start piling up.

Though each of the reasons above may not be the case always, every such fix should be evaluated for its impact to be causing one of the above. If so, care should be taken to replace the quick fix with the right solution at the earliest. Right solutions may be costly to implement in comparison but, in the long term, prove to be the enduring factors.

Examples of *Jugaad* in product development

Let us take a few examples of functionalities required from an application, which is a product being sold as an enterprise service catalog aggregation and service lifecycle management. This product has the feature of service orchestration for automated service delivery and operation integration for task-driven standard service delivery. (For simplicity, let's call it XSM). We would cite possible solutions to these requirements and would like the reader to guess the *jugaad* solutions after evaluating the impact of possible solutions. We successfully avoided the *Jugaad*, as explained in the examples below:

Example 1 -

Use case - On XSM implemented for one enterprise; employee users can check the pricing of service before ordering the service. However, for another enterprise, employee users should not check the pricing of service simply because the chargebacks are not applicable.

Possible Solutions -

1. A feature that controls the visibility of price as per the enterprise it is implemented for.
2. A feature that hides the visibility of price which is 0. Prices for services that need not be shown should be set as 0.
3. A feature that provides a toggle that controls the visibility of price at the instance level.
4. A feature that provides a toggle that controls the visibility of price at the service level and let the data configuration admin decide upon visibility at the service level.

Example 2 -

Use case - On XSM implemented for an enterprise, employee users can mention the date by when a service is required, and those drive an SLA. However, for another enterprise, employee users cannot specify the date, and the same SLA is driven by what the vendor has signed for.

Possible Solutions -

1. A feature that controls the editing of date as per the enterprise it is implemented for.
2. A feature that provides a toggle that controls the editing of date at the instance level.
3. A feature that provides a toggle that controls the editing of date at the service level and let the data configuration admin decide upon editing at the service level.

Example 3 -

Use case - On XSM implemented for an enterprise, orders of one service need to be replicated to another system, which is used by the service vendor to initiate the fulfillment of the order. The other system requires a specific set of data elements to be replicated. Orders of another service need to be replicated to yet another system that is used by another service vendor to initiate the fulfillment of the order. This other system requires a specific set of data elements to be replicated, which are different from the first set.

Possible Solutions -

1. A feature that captures the data to be replicated as per the system it is targeted for can be built in the code.
2. A feature that captures the data to be replicated at the service level and let the data configuration admin decide upon the

data at the service level.

In all the able examples, the common underlying challenge is that if XSM was built for an enterprise, features could have been coded specifically for that enterprise. However, this approach would have worked in case XSM is a bespoke application for the enterprise. What if the app is not bespoke but a COTS product?

Use principals of *Jugaad* but not the goal of *Jugaad*

1. Thrift, not waste. This first rule — which promotes frugality — helps tackle the scarcity of all forms of resources.
2. Inclusion, not exclusion. This second rule helps entrepreneurial organizations to put inclusiveness into practice — by tightly connecting with, and harnessing, the growing diversity that permeates their communities of customers, employees, and partners.
3. Bottom-up participation, not top-down command and control. This third rule drives collaboration.
4. Flexible thinking and action, not linear planning. This fourth rule facilitates exibility in thought and action. *Jugaad*-practicing teams are highly adaptable as they aren't wedded to any single business model and pursue multiple options at any time.

Business Pressure and its impact

Every business has a pressure of competition and the margins. Product manager (and product delivery team that includes designer, developer, tester, QA, etc.) will always be pressured by business to deliver fast and o er a competitive pricing strategy.

It is the job of the product manager to withstand the pressure and make the right decisions. Two crucial points in the common scenarios of business pressure:

1. Not to succumb to the pressure on non-negotiable standards like security
2. Not to remove any feature function from a base product.

We have seen both compromises in the Boeing 737 Max grounding case. The company was in pressure to release the product faster to compete against Airbus 321 Neo that leads to mistakes in the design itself.

According to Indonesian investigators, design and oversight lapses played a central role in the fatal crash of a Boeing 737 MAX jet. Boeing derived the basic designs (primarily the fuselage and wing) from earlier models to make it fast. Enhancements were made on top of that. And the testing was fast-tracked. Further investigation revealed that the FAA delegated authority to the planemaker to assess the safety of certain flight-control features. Because of this delegation, essential design changes did not receive adequate FAA attention.

As per reports, Boeing had admitted that it knew about a problem with its 737 Max jets a year before the aircraft was involved in two fatal accidents but took no action. Boeing said it had unwittingly made an alarm feature optional instead of standard. We also know that the availability of this feature could have very well avoided the accidents because of which the Boeing 737 MAX was grounded worldwide.

The general attitude to produce quality

To produce good quality, you should first learn to reject bad quality, even if it is produced by yourself. It is a matter of attitude. If you do not reject it, your customer will reject it, and that is the worst thing about your product. Sometimes we do make a compromise, and compromises are a tradeoff for a particular situation (and *jugaad* is one of them) but keep the compromises outside the product. Quality is not absolute but always about certain standards. You may have two quality products of different standards. The higher standard may be perceived as higher quality, but that would be a wrong comparison. Take the example of two car manufacturers who manufacture cars for a common segment. The mindset of one car manufacturer could be to set the quality standards first and design the car with the lowest possible price in conformance with the set quality standards. The other car manufacturer's mindset could be to set the price point first and design the best quality confirming to that price point. In both cases, the outcome is quality but of different standards. that is the worst thing about your product.

4.8 Economics of CN applications

We do not intend to provide any guidance and financial management expertise but want to clarify some essential points for awareness.

1. CN application cost of ownership likely to be higher under some circumstances
2. DevOps is more expensive in practice as compared to SDLC
3. Cloud may be more expensive because the software components are increasingly getting resource hungry and nullifying the advantage of decreasing hardware cost
4. Deployment architecture and bearing on the cost

While CN application may scale up because of multiple containers, it may pose a commercial challenge of the price viability for lower scale operation. For example, an application can be designed with four microservices, and the same app can also be designed with twelve microservices. The breakeven point of running twelve containers would be much higher and expect a minimum scale of operation.

Deployment architecture and pricing model of provider

Deployment architecture is the design for the deployment of an application package for performance, security, availability, and other system qualities. In traditional terms, a deployment architecture maps the logical architecture to a physical environment which consists of the computing nodes, processors, memory, storage and its devices, and other hardware and network pieces required. Designing the deployment architecture involves deciding the size needed by the deployment in order to determine the resources necessary to meet the system requirements. The cost of the deployment is assessed after a deployment architecture design is complete. In the Cloud Native world, the physical environment is replaced by the cloud services, and the cost is assessed by the cloud service consumed and metering and billing model of those services. Metering for APIs and services is quite different than the metering and billing for virtual infrastructure in the cloud.

5 CORNERSTONE OF CLOUD NATIVITY

5.1 Microservice Architecture

Microservice architecture style has caught the fancy of software developers and architects and is now being seen as more and more appealing for modern application development. Even though inter-process communication is not a new thing, the popularity of the architecture since it came in the reckoning in 2011 has got pronounced in the last two years with Cloud Native application development picking up pace. In this architecture, the application is a composite of services, each running in its separate process. Each service is required to perform a specific responsibility and is an application that is needed to provide services to the composite application that utilizes these services. The microservices interact with each other either through messaging protocols or Rest calls over HTTP.

A microservice is a service serving to a large complex application. It is built to serve a small purpose in the larger and complex application that it serves. However, it is still an application in its own right built to the specifications of the language in which it is developed. An application may consist of microservices, each of which may be written in a different language. All it requires is the availability of the required runtime on the cloud to run that application.

Microservice has similarities to Service Oriented Architecture in terms of providing services for use by external applications but is vastly different. The difference lies in various facets, as mentioned below:

1. A microservice is for a single purpose that does one thing well.
2. Microservices do not share. Therefore, there is no relying on other services.
3. Microservices have an API layer or simple messaging between services and service consumers and not messaging middleware.
4. Changing a microservice is far easier as it is smaller in its purpose.
5. Microservice serves multiple other microservices that are part of the same application.

Designing a microservice is an art that not many get right for the first time. The design should not lead to adding constituents more than what is required. However, this very decision of what is needed and what is not is driven by what business objective a microservice is expected to meet and is fraught with errors. Each microservice should ideally have its database, but there could be cases where database sharing should be allowed because there is too much to share, and rather than keeping disparate, the choice would be to have one database shared. An example is when you have multiple services looking to access the same data in real-time. The microservices can communicate with each other synchronously as well as asynchronously again weighed in by business requirements of whether real-time communication is required or not. Depending upon the need, the communications could be Rest based, or message-based brought in through publish or subscribe messaging models.

5.1.1 Advantages

Microservices architecture brings about lots of advantages. As each service lives independently, it is possible to have the services deployable, upgradable, replaceable, and scalable independent of each other. Faster development is likely because you have separate teams working on separate codebases. It is possible to have different technology stack as it is the service contract that rules inter-service communication and thus, there is no constraint to have the same language throughout. It gives the development teams to pursue the development in their own choice of languages. Fault identification is quicker as each service is designed to do some specific things only. Also, integration of code is easier as it gets delivered, resulting in faster and more reliable continuous delivery and deployment of large and complex applications. Since there are multiple codebases, it is easier to add features.

5.1.2 Pre-requisites

Adoption of microservices architecture should be decided upon after careful assessment of your environment on the following:

1. The application should have been modeled based on the business domain it is a part of. There should be a strong understanding of the business domain that is being modeled. Thanks to object-oriented programming that we all know well, we already know what this signifies. But what we need to be careful is that there need to be right boundaries defining the application components that should be modeled around different business capabilities.

There should be a definite scope of each component and the interfaces that it would serve as well as require. Loosely defined interfaces and lack of clarity on scope and boundaries do not bode well for a microservice. Microservice architecture is an evolution of the design of the application and not the initial step. Application complexity defines the need for having microservices.

2. The components should be highly mutable. The application is evolving, and as it grows, its components would need continuous changes in architecture and deployment. You need to fail fast to have still time to find another approach.

3. The team can be structured as per the application model. The business function alignment of the team is necessary. Your teams need to be self-contained in terms of DevOps support, including business analysts who can identify the bounded context(s), as well as support for monitoring and testing, i.e., you have a healthy DevOps culture in your organization. The team should own the service it is responsible for - Building as well as maintaining.

4. Support for multiple databases in your application, including different types of databases with different kinds of data-stores.

5. The pH of the distributed transaction processing or consistency model to be moved from ACID to BaSE form. It is because every microservice will have its database with different types of data stores or polyglot persistence.

6. The development team possesses skills of adding and maintaining ReST and messaging-based communication layers. Developers should continue honoring the API

contracts their service is signed for while programming.

7. A platform that manages the infrastructure and addresses the cross-cutting concerns.

8. A comprehensive testing strategy that covers functional, integration, and performance assessments.

9. Fault tolerance is essential for availability - understand that microservices architecture introduces multiple points of failure in your application, and you will have to add components to absorb failures like circuit breakers, configuration server, client-side load balancers, and service registry.

5.1.3 Challenges and Remediation

1. Having microservices is not for the sake of having. Also, having too many microservices will introduce latency and risk getting into overlapping data situations. Do not start with a microservice – always begin with building a monolith and be sensitive to the point when to break it. The point of breaking could either be having too many transactions, or a component requiring a refactoring, or a component requiring a different roadmap of evolution. Incision leading to a microservice should have clear cut boundaries - Clear and bounded context is a must.

2. Discoverability of services – Since the cloud infrastructure is mutable, the services should be reconfigured dynamically. Your service should be quickly discoverable when a new service instance is created. Services register themselves in a service registry that other services utilize to discover the services.

3. Load Balancing – Brought in for distributing loads between two instances of the same service.

4. Failure handling - Circuit breakers ensure that connections to a service instance are snapped if there are multiple failures over the defined threshold limit in calling a service instance. It is done to maintain the health of the application. In case of multiple failures, the circuit is made open, and all subsequent calls to the instance are snapped. Instead, the fallback mechanism is activated.

5. Direct chats - Consider using a gateway to avoid coding and refactoring complexities as well as to ensure protocol compatibilities.

6. Testing gaps - Your testing strategy should be comprehensive - Unit, Integration, Contract, End-to-end, and Performance.

7. Choice of too much – Take nothing more than what you require to minimize risks associated with later changes in definition.

8. Latency - Abandon the microservice if the functionality is performance-critical, hugely transactional across application boundaries, and any lag introduced because of communication across boundaries will not be acceptable to the business.

9. Precise definitions - Be mindful of the fact that you cannot have services defined right always, and you may have to change your service definitions a lot of times before you could finally have well-defined services with zero or minimal overlap. Depending on the perceived frequency of

changes, business capability(s) being tried to address, clarity in the definition of interfaces, and dependencies and overlaps in functionality and data being stored, you may also have to merge two services into one.

10. Lightweight communications - Communications are substantial between microservices. Lightweight protocols like AMQP or Http need to be used for communications. REST API calls and JSON payloads or message exchanges off a queue or event bus can be used to facilitate the communication. The communications protocols used for microservice interactions within the same node or cluster, as well as interactions with external services using APIs enable composition, access management, and enforcing usage limits.

11. Fast scale-ups - Apart from cloud provider support, the stateless design of microservice aids in rapid scaling up.

12. Multiple runtimes - An application environment needs to support multiple languages to create new services or to help port or extend the application. Developers should be allowed to choose the best technology for service as well as work in the technologies they are comfortable with.

While this architectural style is one of the tenets of cloud nativity, these are two separate concepts, and having one does not mean you have the other. At the same time, it is true that as cloud adoption is increasing, microservices are becoming increasingly popular.

Are monoliths bad?

While having a microservices-based architecture has a lot of advantages, it does not mean that a monolith application is not a Cloud Native application. Even a monolith application follows all twelve factors, is characterized by DevOps, Containers, and CI/CD mechanism. Let us see the differences in a bit more detail between monoliths and microservices.

In microservices, the application is split into a set of smaller, interconnected services. The application complexity is divided into a set of manageable services faster to develop and easier to understand and maintain. Each service can be developed & deployed independently, making simultaneous deployments possible. It allows each service to be scaled separately. It reduces the barrier to adopting new technologies and is suited for complex domain applications.

In monoliths, the application is built into a single entity and codebase. The application construct is too large and complex to understand and make changes fast and correctly thoroughly. It requires deploying the entire application making continuous deployment difficult. It is difficult to scale when different modules have conflicting resource requirements. The changes in frameworks or languages affect the whole application. The architecture is suited for simple, lightweight applications.

So, is there a choice at all on having a monolith vs. having a microservice-based architecture for a complex application? The answer is Yes and No. Yes, when you are starting with your application. If multiple functions are clearly defined, there can be components that can be clearly defined centered on serving those functions. Microservices should be a clear choice to start here. But otherwise, only once the components start having a distinct scope and interfaces, monolith should be considered to break into microservices. In our product journey, we started with a monolith and then cut it into microservices later with the expansion of functionalities.

5.2 12-Factor App Methodology

The Twelve-factor app is a methodology for building software-as-a -service apps. These are a set of rules that guide the building of Cloud Native applications. These rules form a contract between an application and the cloud management platform that helps the applications leverage the cloud infrastructure and its services. It was initially developed by engineers at Heroku for various applications built on the Heroku platform and was later adapted to become a baseline for all applications that are meant to be deployed on cloud and is a measure of cloud-nativity of an application. These were presented first by Adam Wiggins in 2011.

The objectives to achieve by having an app adhere to these twelve rules are the following, as described on http://12factor.net. We have elaborated upon each of these to help our readers understand these in simple language.

1. Use declarative formats to setup automation, to minimize time and cost for new developers joining the project - This means that app deployment should be automated, thus implying that twelve-factor apps are built for rapid deployment and hence agility.

2. Have a clean contract with the underlying operating system, offering maximum portability between execution environments - This means that the app should be de-coupled from the underlying operating systems implying that twelve-factor apps can be moved from one execution environment to another.

3. Applications are suitable for deployment on modern cloud platforms, obviating the need for servers and systems administration - Modern cloud platforms sit above the infrastructure/IaaS layer and leverage it directly. Platforms provide the necessary abstraction in utilizing the infrastructure services and manage the application life cycle.

4. Minimize divergence between development and production, enabling continuous deployment for maximum agility - The application is continuously deployed on the cloud, implying that twelve-factor apps have limited or just a few differences between development and production systems.

5. Scale-up without significant changes to tooling, architecture, or development practices - This means that twelve-factor apps can scale up on their own by being on the cloud without requiring any significant change to tooling, architecture or development practices.

5.3 Applying 12-Factor App Methodology

We will guide on how to apply the twelve factors to an app while also referring to what it mandates. While doing so, we will refrain from describing the factor as there is a lot of description already published and available generally on these factors.

Codebase

Each deployable app has a single code base. A version control system tracks the revisions to the codebase.

One needs to create a repository for the code as a library, publish it to Git, Github, Mercurial, or subversion, and integrate using Maven, or Gradle, or any other similar tool you prefer. There is essentially no need to track the source code in revision control to use a cloud platform. However, a revision control system makes you run automated deployments from a central codebase shared by various developers when working as a team. Please be sure to create a .ignore file which tells the files that should not be included when pushing the code to the repo. At a minimum, these are dependent library packages and log files that get built with your app.

What you need to be careful about is that one app should have one codebase. Multiple versions in Production of the same app can run on multiple codebases, but attempts should be made not to have more than three versions in circulation. Please note that this does not include mismatches between Development, Test, and Production environments. Environmental differences arise because of new functionalities brought in through your DevOps cycle, and continuous deployment ensures that your Development, Test, and Production environments are finally synchronized.

Most of the time, the circumstances require us to have separate codebases - branched or forked because of requirements that are considered peculiar. However, every attempt should be made to standardize the functionality and have a single codebase available for all deployments of the application. If at all, the peculiarity of features does not allow bringing them to a single codebase; it is safe to assume that you have created another app.

Points to note:

- If there are multiple codebases, it's not for one application.

- Each component in a distributed system is an application itself
- Each application can individually comply with twelve -factors.
- Multiple apps cannot share the same codebase.
- Better to factor shared code into libraries
- One application many deploys (running instances)
- Different versions may be active in different deploys

Dependencies

Dependencies should not be declared in the codebase. The dependencies need to be declared separately in a file called manifest and should use dependency management tools like npm, maven, Gradle, etc. to get the required dependencies from a library server.

Example: For a Node.js app, dependencies are declared in the app's package.json file like the following:

```
"dependencies": {
        "axios": "0.19.0",
        "body-parser": "1.19.0",
        "cfenv": "1.2.2",
        "cloudant": "*",
        "express": "4.17.1",
        "json2csv": "*"
    }
```

Cloud platforms install dependencies on deployment and use cache for repeat deployments.

Points to note:

- Explicitly declare and isolate dependencies
- Never rely on the implicit existence of system-wide

packages
- Ensure that no implicit dependencies "leak in" from the surrounding system
- Dependency declaration and isolation must always be used together
- Do not rely on the implied existence of any system tools
- Tools will not exist on all the systems where the app may run in the future (or compatible versions will exist on all systems).
- If the app needs to invoke a system tool, it should be embedded in the app as an OEM component.

Configurations

The configuration that is likely to differ between deployment environments (e.g., development, staging, production) should be available to the app as environment variables.

Examples: Services connection strings and credentials, Host names, IPs, database connection properties.

These variables can be available either through operating system level or application properties. Configuration can be changed to make the application run in a deployment environment. Configuration should not be declared as variables in the code. Even though cloud platforms allow defining the environment variables as part of the deployment of an app, the configuration can additionally be made available through environment files like .config, .yml, .json, .properties, .env but having the environment files in app's code repo is still a bad practice.

Points to note:
- Store configuration in the environment

- Strict separation of config from code.
    - Config varies substantially across deploys; code does not
    - Think as if you are making codebase for open source
- Store config in environment variables
- Environment variables are a language- and OS-agnostic standard
    - They are easy to change between two deployments without requiring to change any code
    - They have a lesser chance of getting into the code repo. Unlike custom config files, or other config mechanisms such as Java System Properties, they are language- and OS-agnostic standard.

Backing Services

Databases or message brokers, are treated as backing or infrastructure resources and consumed identically across all environments.

Example: An application that uses the messaging services; if there is a change in the messaging server, only the configurations need to change.

The cloud platform generally offers various services for the applications that are built on that platform. New services can be created and bound to the app from within the platform. Optionally, you can declare the service instances for your app using the manifest.

Remember, there should be no change in the application code

upon change of service.

Points to note:

- Treat backing services as attached resources.
- Each distinct backing service is a resource
- The same system's administrators may locally manage some backing services as the app's runtime deploy and some managed by third parties.
- The app does not differentiate between local and third party services. To the app, those are attached resources accessed via a URL or other locator/credentials stored in the configuration.

Build, Release and Run

The stages of building the deployable package of the app, and its dependencies, and then combining it with configuration, and starting one or more processes from that combination, should be strictly separated.

The build stage takes code from repos and downloads the dependencies before building the bundle of execution. It is the stage where all the unit tests should pass, and failure should mean no further processing unless addressed. The build stage runs automatically as the code is pushed into the code repo by the developers.

The release stage combines the environment variables with the bundle of execution and assigns a release number before making the combination ready to execute on an environment.

The run stage runs the package using the commands.

Points to note:

- Deployments that follow the above run with no manual intervention and execute fast.
- Strictly separate build and run stages. Impossible to make changes to code at run time. Possible to roll back.
- Keep the run stage to as few moving parts as possible. Builds stage is usually complex and initiated by the app's developers. Runtime execution can happen automatically.

Processes

The app processes are stateless and share nothing. The data which needs to persist is necessary to be externalized to backing services, e.g., database, cache, object store, etc.

In the cloud, due to auto-scaling, application instances can automatically grow, and the data in the execution memory cannot be relied on to persist as a restart can erase such data.

Example: Memcached or Redis can be used to store session information.

Points to note:

- The app should execute as one or more stateless processes
- Twelve-factor processes are stateless and do not share anything.
- The data to be persisted must be stored in a stateful backing service
- The memory space or file system of the process can be used as a brief, single-transaction cache
- Never assume that anything cached in memory or on disk will be available on a future request or job.
- Do not use or rely on sticky sessions.

Port Binding

The app is self-contained. It exports services via port binding and listens to the requests coming on that port.

Ports that can be exposed are governed by the cloud service provider to prevent malicious code from connecting or reaching out with unsupported protocols, and for keeping inbound network traffic compliant with the platform's routing capabilities.

Points to note:

- Export services via port binding.
- The twelve-factor app is completely self-contained
- Does not rely on runtime injection of a webserver into the execution environment
- Exports HTTP as a service by binding to a port
- It is the primary instrument for orchestration.
- One app can be a backing service for another app through the port it exposes.

Concurrency

Scale-out app processes horizontally. Avoid building a single large application; instead, look to have a multi-process application with each process being independently scalable. Instead of having processes multiplex work via app managed threads as it may hit the sealing on a vertical scale, additional process instances must be added to an application. The manifest file contains the memory to be allocated to a process and the number of processes to be created.

Example:
applications:

```
- name: hello app
  memory: 512M
  instances: 1
```

Disposability

Processes should start up quickly and shut down gracefully. It allows for rapid elastic scaling and deployment of changes. Ports are set free, and the system is left in the right state upon a graceful shutdown. It also ensures rapid recovery from crashes. The application robustness increases if the processes or backing services can start up quickly upon failures.

Example: Consider a banking site that has services like authentication, funds transfer, cheque-book ordering, etc. The failure of any service should be quickly retractable by a quick startup of the failed service.

Points to note:

- Maximize robustness with fast startup and graceful shutdown
- Allows rapid recovery

Dev production parity

Keep the deployment environments as similar as possible. The differences between Dev and Prod beyond the configuration and data can grow significantly over time. A developer may have worked on code that took weeks to go into production. Also, the developers write code while Ops engineers deploy it. There could also be a case where developers may be using a different set of tools than in production.

To avoid these problems, twelve-factor apps should be continuously deployed by keeping development, staging, and production environments as similar as possible. It avoids unknown errors that can be seen when the application is deployed in a new environment.

Logs

Logs should be treated as streams. Do not use log files. Logs seen as event streams allow the execution environment to collect, aggregate, and analyze the events via log management services.

Example - Logs can be aggregated by tools like Splunk or Logstash/ELK Stack to help with analysis.

Admin

Administrative or management tasks should be executed as one-off processes. Consider a job such as a database script, which needs to run every time a new app instance is created. It is easiest done by having the admin code with the application code. The script can be made part of an automated process which is not part of the standard execution of the service. For example: In a Node.js app, add an install script to the package.json file.

```
{
 ...
 "scripts": {
  "install": "./admin.js dbddl"
 },
 ...
}
```

5.4 Other Important factors

The twelve factors mentioned above have become the design principles for any application, whether it's a new one being considered to be built on cloud or a legacy application being considered for migration to the cloud. As mentioned before, the twelve principles are a measure of the cloud nativity of an application. However, three other factors are important but are not part of the original twelve. Let us look at these now.

API First/Code to Contract

Application is a mix of services that are provided or consumed by various application components generally modeled on a business domain. The components get manifested in the app through services that interact with each other through interfaces without needing to know the specific details about each other. Therefore, there must be well-defined interfaces that other services can use to utilize a service. An interface becomes a contract that exists between two services for information exchange. Any time the agreement is altered, service communication is bound to get broken. The development, therefore, needs to code not to break any existing interface or contract.

Telemetry/Measurements

Real-time view of the application health and other parameters is essential to understand how the application is behaving in the cloud. Being on the cloud, access to an application instance is only through the codebase used for build and deployment. However, to understand the behavior of the application while in the deployed state, it is crucial to define the parameters that will be measured. Generally, third-party tools or cloud platform services are used to measure and monitor these. The metrics would include the following:

1. Application health status - whether the application instance is available or not.
2. Application performance - define the time within which a specific number of transactions systems should be able to complete. For example, you want to measure the time in which a user can order and cancel an existing order after the submit or cancel button is clicked.
3. Business-specific - define what you need to measure as per your business needs. For example, you want to measure how many times a user has logged in the past month.
4. System Logs - Cloud platform provider provides the logging services. The logs tell what is happening in the system. Both application logs and system-component logs are aggregated, simplifying their ingestion. A metrics collector gathers and streams metrics from the system components. Operators can use metrics to monitor an application instance. Logs can be viewed from the command line or drained into a log management service.

Security

Security should be a factor to be considered at multiple layers and is of prime concern right from the beginning of app development even during the making of the choice of cloud services vendor right till the end of life of the application. Application security is a continuous aspect that needs to be considered. It encompasses the following layers:

- Infrastructure
- Platform
- Application DevOps

- Application
- Data

While few aspects of security are built-in as those are provided as a service or are embedded in services from cloud providers, others are either essential add-ons or optional add-ons.
Let us look at each of the layers now in greater detail and look at typical built-ins and add-ons.

Infrastructure Security

Physical Security - Security of physical infrastructure and facilities where the infrastructure is hosted are offered as built-in services from the cloud services provider. It includes - perimeter, physical entry controls in offices, rooms, facilities, building, utilities, cables, utility equipment, physical assets like servers and devices, human resources, etc.

Network Security - Security of the underlying network is a mix of built-in and optional add ons. Built-in security controls include – network isolation, connectivity, segmentation, firewalls, IDS, IPS, DDoS protection. Add ons include direct links, VPN, VPN/IPSec tunnel.

Platform Security

Cloud services providers are responsible for the following:
- managing OS vulnerabilities
- implementing role-based access controls in accessing platform services
- preventing possible denial-of-service attacks

- securing code and the configuration of an application
- managing vulnerabilities in platform services
- isolating containers
- providing audit trails on operator actions
- implementing network traffic rules
- security monitoring and intelligence at the platform level
- secured containers

Application DevOps

The application should be engineered with strong security and privacy controls while running on the cloud. The DevOps teams should take the concerns and risks related to the security of the application very seriously and should always be looking to increase the adoption of security practices in the DevOps cycle. The application should utilize multiple security controls that the cloud offers, and DevOps practices should build upon these security controls. Let us look at various security practices that can be followed concerning the engineering, deployment, and operations of an application.

1. Requirements and Design: For every new business requirement, user security and system security requirements get identified and defined. The design of these requirements should align with the security controls available in the application. The design should also seek to utilize the application security controls offered by the cloud provider. Examples of such controls are:

a. Identity and Access Management - User authentication enabled through SAML and OAuth.
b. Data Security – both for data at rest and in motion.
c. Object Storage used to store media files and user-provided file attachments

d. Secured CI/CD Pipelines
e. Container security to ensure isolation and authorized access
f. Vulnerability and patch management of cloud platform
g. Build-pack updates

2. Developer Education: Guidelines covering vulnerabilities arising out of technical and business logic aspects should be reviewed from time to time, and developer awareness on these should be ensured. These vulnerabilities follow recommendations of the Open Web Application Security Project (OWASP), as well as technology-specific security guidance.

3. Coding Practices: To ensure software quality and coding standards for security, guidelines should be implemented through linters. Code review based on Quality Profiles built around application security needs to be conducted through tools that run on Developer IDE as well as get embedded in CI/CD pipelines. Third-party services can be used to identify and mitigate security risks in open source application components. These scan for newly introduced open source and helps manage security vulnerabilities.

4. Security Testing: Third-party services can be used for the Dynamic Application Security Testing (DAST) Tool to detect security vulnerabilities. The scan should be conducted after every major release on the application or on-demand, whichever is earlier, to ensure there are no new vulnerabilities introduced since fixing of last scan vulnerabilities because of any code changes on account of new features or bug fixes. The development team should analyze all issues and recommendations from the testing tool and resolve and distribute the fixes for security defects

and vulnerabilities.

5. Deployment: DevOps ensures that the security tests are a pre-requisite and should be without any open Critical and Major vulnerabilities for every candidate for deployment before a decision on deployment is taken. Besides, only authorized DevOps personnel need to have access to:
   a. CI/CD pipelines - Differentiated access based on deployment environment and ability to edit or run a pipeline. No manual intervention is required on deployment scripts to run a pipeline.
   b. Production and Staging branches of code repo
   c. Production and Staging instances of the app
   d. Production and Staging Databases - Differentiated access based on the deployment environment. No manual intervention is required on deployment scripts to migrate a database from one environment to another.

Application Security

Following security controls should be built in the application:

- Identity and Access Management - Authentication and Authorization controls need to be made to ensure only the right user gets access only to something which he or she is entitled to.
- User authentication - Instrumented through cloud provided authentication mechanism
- User authorization - role-based access control mechanism
- User entitlements
- Encrypted and signed sessions
- Session invalidation
- Record level auditing
- Activity Logs

Data Security

The data life cycle in any application defines the various phases of data from its creation and storage to its deletion. Security is at the core of all the phases and is explained below.

- Create - Data should be created/uploaded through a secured network channel.
- Store - Data should be stored on the cloud and secured through encryption, database activity monitoring, deployment hardening, and secure design principles provided by the vendor. Encryption services should be used for data at rest and backups.
- Transact - Data transaction/data in motion should be secured over SSL. All the application transactions should be secured through SSL.
- Archive/Backup - Data should be archived at regular intervals to maintain the performance in the or a different database.
- Destroy - Data should be securely and permanently deleted. All the backups and archival tables should also be removed permanently.
- Data Isolation - While data is stored in the cloud, the cloud vendor should provide complete isolation of the data using containerization. This way, data is kept separate and isolated.

Application Interfaces

The interface allows the exchange of information between one IT system and another system. An application implements two interfaces - Programming and User Interface.

APIs: Application Programming Interface (API) is an interface between parts of an application program or two applications. An API can be used to provide functionality or access to data from an application so that the data and functionality can be accessed by another app that makes the requests to the API. Simply put, it is the code that allows two software programs to communicate with each other.

APIs serve the purpose of communication between two applications by accessing data and functionality of one application from another application. With this, the need for APIs has grown in the cloud world. APIs now also serve to meet complex business needs that require one application to access multiple applications by linking applications in an ecosystem of various applications. APIs have led to something called digitized assets, which are the functionality pieces which can be accessed programmatically from outside. There are companies in the world that have monetized these assets by charging the calls or requests to APIs that they have built. API can be accessed by the outside world to make use of the API to develop and create new applications. APIs can also be used internally to maximize the reuse and enforce consistency in the application behavior.

Since an API is a broker to the functionality and data access from an application, the application developers need to make sure that the API is designed and built well to fit the needs of communicating with the application it belongs to. If an API is incorrectly designed and constructed, the cost of replacement is huge. Let us look at the API design factors now:

- API design should make the API simple to use and should be iteratively designed to meet the developer response obtained from time to time.

- The specific use case should guide the API design meant to serve, rather than the design of the application itself.
- API design should meet the response time requirements from API calls.
- API access should be secured as per the security requirements.
- Provide only as much data as required and hide the complexities of the application it is built on.

There should be strong governance around any design change of an API.

Graphic User Interface (GUI)

It is a type of interface that allows users to interact with applications through visual indicators like graphical icons, buttons, scroll bars, checkboxes, menus, etc. It is the main thing with which the user interacts with the application. The access to GUI is through hardware, which can be a touch screen, mouse, microphone, or a keyboard.

GUI and API: Differences

GUI	API
Interface designed for a human user to interact with an application / software	Interface designed for an application/software to use another application/software

Key considerations- Content, color scheme, visual control, action button, layout appearance, visual design, the action buttons	Key considerations - Parameters, methods, data structures
Enabling considerations - information architecture, site mapping, natural flow	Enabling considerations - Simplicity of use, developer looking to consume API understands its response values
Makes use of HTML, CSS to render the interface elements like buttons, menus, etc.	It is accessible through URLs.
Can invoke APIs by sending user requests to the API URLs	Makes use of handler functions that issue actions when they receive requests from a user.
GUI security is encapsulated in application security	API security has to be implemented, just like application security.

GUI is the visual layer that rides over the application layer	API can itself be an application
The user interface is generally constrained by the client capabilities even though efforts should be made to design GUI to support more extensive accessibility, e.g., GUI of web applications is usually limited by browser versions and so capabilities. But care should be taken to keep the GUI accessible across a broad browser spectrum.	The type of client does not limit API use as the response of all APIs is either in XML or JSON format.
The size of the graphic elements drives performance.	The processing time drives performance.

Operating System Services to SOAP to REST

Operating system services are the predecessor of the API concept. Many capabilities of an operating system are available to the operating system services. For example, if a developer has to present a dialog box on the screen or a resizable pop up for data collection, then he or she need not write the code of doing so. The developer can use Windows OS services. For different applications developed by different developers, the dialog box capability might work differently as per each programmer's and use case's requirement of how such windows should look and feel. While Microsoft offers Windows as an operating system, it also provides developers with APIs to draw those windows on the screen with only a few lines of code.

SOAP (Simple Object Access Protocol) came into existence during Web and Internet evolution. It is primarily a messaging protocol for exchanging structured information in the implementation of web services. It uses XML as the messaging format and relies on other protocols, most often Hypertext Transfer Protocol (HTTP) and Simple Mail Transfer Protocol (SMTP), for messaging. Popular web protocols like HTTP and SMTP are standards across all systems; SOAP allows application clients to call web services and receive responses independent of language and platforms.

REST (Representational State Transfer) is a web services API that is based on URIs (Uniform Resource Identifier, identifiers of the resource being requested) requested over HTTP and supports JSON as the default format for data exchange, which is compatible with all modern browsers. It could also use the SOAP protocol, but in doing so, it will lose simplicity and lightweight. REST APIs are simple to build and scale, but they can be massive and complicated—it is all in how they are built, added on to, and what they are designed to do.

SOAP is a protocol, and REST is an architectural style. A REST

API can utilize the SOAP protocol, just like it can use HTTP. That means both could be differently packaged, have different functions, and be used in different scenarios. It is like mailing an envelope vs. mailing a postcard. SOAP is like sending an envelope that carries an extra overhead, requires more bandwidth, and needs extra work at both ends. REST APIs are lightweight, can be cached, and are easy to update.

Are REST APIs good enough?

Constraints of Statelessness: Because of HTTP, REST makes the interactions of client and server stateless. The server does not store anything about the HTTP request the client made. It will treat each request as new, no data of previous session- no session data and no history, and no client context can be stored on the server between requests. However, for the end-user, the application needs to be stateful, i.e., the user should log-in once and perform authorized operations after that. To enable this, each request from the client should contain what is required by the server to fulfill the request, i.e., authentication and authorization details. The client, thus, in a way, should manage the state of the application.

Constraints of cacheability: Caching eliminates some client-server interactions and helps to improve performance and scalability. In REST, resources have to declare themselves cacheable. The caching can be implemented on the server or client-side.

Constraints of a uniform interface: REST means a single API interface for a resource inside the system which is exposed to API consumers. A resource should have one URI that should provide an interface to fetch related or additional data.

API security

Traditional security tools focus has been around having on-premise applications and deal with conventional attacks like SQL injection and a cross-eyed scripting attack. However, the most common cause of data breach that is happening in the modern world is an API sitting behind million-plus records that have now been stolen or accessed illegally. Therefore, it is important to secure resources exposed by API by securing access to the API. Ways to secure APIs could be:

1. Define clear access rights for each user accessing the API
2. API needs to enforce authentication and authorization. Tokens can be assigned to establish identities. Signatures can be used to verify that the sender is who they say they are.
3. Maintain audits of API access as well as actions performed through API.
4. Encryption using TLS allows communications to be securely encrypted.
5. Third-party packages or components that are used in an API should be kept up to date.
6. Use an API Gateway to enforce policies on the API access.

5.5 Dependency hell

Modern software projects depend on other software packages, including the operating system libraries, to provide functionality. The larger a software project is, the more the possibilities are of a large number of dependencies either internally between different parts of the code or externally with third-party libraries. Dependency hell is an adverse situation that occurs when these dependencies break the functionalities of the core application software that is a software application is not able to access those functionalities it requires to work.

JAR hell or classpath hell or dll hell are dependency hell's common and similar terminologies, and these include software performing abnormally, or with bugs, or error messages, or stopping functioning. At times, the software dependencies are brought in by the use of third party components.

Key reasons that lead to the dependency hell include

1. A chain of dependencies or dependencies between values in the same table. For an application to work, it would need a limited number of libraries. Each of those libraries, in turn, might need some other libraries, and so on. As the problem of unexpressed dependencies is multiplied, it becomes exponentially more labor-intensive and error-prone.
2. Conflicting programs that require different versions of a third library. If different versions are present on the classpath, the behavior will be unpredictable.
3. The core application requirement creates circular dependencies. It is the closed-loop case of transitive dependency, where the dependency chain loops back to the originating library and is a vicious circle.
4. Installations of a package directly from package installers. Package managers take care of upgrading the dependent packages simultaneously. However, an upgrade of dependency in case of the directly installed package can lead to breakage of other package calls which are made from the upgraded package

The Cloud Native environment is by design an immutable infrastructure and provides ways to avoid the dependency problems and uncontrolled changes.

Impact on Cloud Native applications

One of the messengers of Cloud Native computing is a microservices architecture, and by now, we know that a single Cloud Native application can be a composite of small services catered to meet specific business requirements. Each service runs in its process, and the application is dependent on inter-process communication. New features can lead to the addition of new services and new libraries. Precisely here is where the dependency hell can impact the application. The hell can break the communications between microservices leading to situations that drive you to consider going back to monolithic architecture. There are three symptoms of hell, gripping up your microservices architecture:

1. Newer services are being added, which are just a little different from the existing ones. It could be leading to the addition of more modern libraries.
2. Newer APIs being created with little consideration to utilize the existing ones with tweaks.
3. Services that are heavily dependent on a few other services. Failure of one could lead to the failure of dependent ones.

These symptoms could further be leading to an avoidable increase in the amount of code, thus causing a reduction of code quality and misplaced development efforts.

Avoiding Hell

Let us now see design considerations as well as measures that can be taken to eliminate the hell situations.

1. Database separation - All microservices should have

Using Open Source Components

The use of open-source software and copyright infringement is a big problem to address. Not only it is easy to infringe on intellectual property rights, but also it is harder to prevent others from stealing IP.
Open JDK available through GPL, Docker available through Apache, Kubernetes, Eclipse IDE are some of the examples.

Copyright vs. Copyleft

A copyright is a legal right of the creator of original works that allows the creator to dictate how those works can or cannot be copied, modified, and distributed by others. The creator can seek legal action If someone violates the terms and conditions set by the creator. The main idea behind copyright is that creators restrict what others can or cannot do with their works and must grant individual permission to do otherwise.

Copyleft licenses remain within the legal boundary of copyrights, and it does not abolish copyrights. Copyleft licenses are a subset of copyright licenses and aim to provide freedom to users. The core concept of copyleft is that users should have the right to freely use, copy, modify, and distribute works however they want, with one crucial clause: all derivative works must offer the same freedoms to users. The GNU General Public License (GNU GPL or GPL) is a widely-used free software license, which guarantees end users the freedom to run, study, share, and modify the software. The most important aspect of copyleft licenses is that they require users to distribute derivative works under a license that offers the same rights as the original work. The "share-alike" clause that maintains freedom in derivative works.

Copyleft is not always free

You might not be able to acquire a specific copyleft work without first paying for it. But once you do pay for it, you are free to modify and distribute as long as you maintain the same copyleft freedoms in the derived work. Red Hat Enterprise Linux is an excellent practical example of this. The Linux kernel is licensed under the GNU General Public License (GPL), which is a copyleft license. Red Hat Enterprise Linux (RHEL) is a commercial operating system built on a modified Linux kernel. The desktop version of RHEL is sold for $49, but to abide by the GPL, the RHEL source code is included in the purchase. RHEL users are free to modify and redistribute the source code, which is how the free RHEL-clone operating system called CentOS came about. However, users are not allowed to resell RHEL itself because a trademark protects RHEL.

6.1 Development environment on PaaS

Platform as a service (PaaS) provides the development and deployment environment in the cloud that enables developers to build and deploy Cloud Native applications. PaaS platforms drive the underlying infrastructure and related services. These platforms sit above the infrastructure layer and leverage it directly on behalf of the application. They also offer services for managing the entire application life cycle. Apart from infrastructure services like servers, storage, and networking, these platforms also provide middleware, development tools, business intelligence, database management services, and many more. PaaS is designed to support the management of the application lifecycle: building, testing, deploying, managing, and updating. The enterprises are responsible only to manage the application and its services. PaaS provides the platform on which developers can build and deploy applications. Examples of PaaS services are - Heroku, Google App Engine, and IBM Cloud.

IDE on PaaS

Traditionally, IDEs to write and test software used to be installed on the developer's machine. Most of the traditional IDEs have now got cloud versions that allow developers to connect to the IDE on the cloud rather than through installations on local machines. The PaaS providers have also started to provide IDEs on a cloud though those are still maturing as compared to traditional IDEs. However, an interesting point to note is that while developers have got more empowered through PaaS, there are a plethora of services on PaaS that they now have to run through to identify the right service for use. The toolset on PaaS is driven towards not only building and deploying applications as it is on IaaS but also towards utilizing the additional services that PaaS has to offer as those provide a lot of value. We have no hesitation in terming this combined environment of toolset and services as Integrated Cloud Development and Deployment Environment or ICDDE.

ICDDE allows developers to benefit from automated self-service provisioning of runtime resources, container technologies, and utilization and monitoring of value-adding services. It is proven and integrated to offer a wide choice of standard and familiar languages and frameworks, automation of containers, and a market place of services. Developers are focused on building applications with an assurance that the platform takes care of operations and infrastructure.

The marketplace of services on ICDDE provides an ecosystem

of vendors offering technologies that cover application, data, and mobile services, including testing and hands-on experience. An app can utilize a service by binding the service to the app. It is done automatically, thus eliminating the complexities around deployment and resource management. A development team should be able to have a quick start with the technology stack that it finds best suited for its apps and look to fast convert new ideas into complex applications, thus increasing business agility. In case a service is not available on PaaS, those can always be taken from outside the marketplace and accessed over the cloud.

ICDDE thus automates complete DevOps cycle whereas an IDE is limited to be a code editor, a compiler, a debugger, a build automation tool with plugins to write better code and pull or push code from or to a code repository. The ICDDE gets tied to the PaaS on which it works best; however, IDE is cloud-agnostic. It is perceived as vendor lock-in for DevOps automation but is still acceptable because the runtime is anyways agnostic from any cloud vendor.

ICDDE Examples:

DevOps phase	IBM	Pivotal	App Engine
PaaS	Cloud Foundry	Cloud Foundry	App Engine
Source Code Repository	GitHub, GitLab	GitHub, GitLab	Cloud Source Repository
Organize and Plan	Gitlab Issues	CloudForge Bugs, Issues, Wikis	Usually third-party tools like Jira

Build, Continuous Integration, and Deployment	Runtimes, Delivery Pipeline, Globalization Pipeline, Auto-scaling	Runtimes, Concourse, App Autoscaler	Cloud Build, Cloud Deployment Manager
Logging	logDNA	Splunk, Fluentd	Stackdriver Log Storage
Performance Tests	Blazemeter, Load Impact	Blazemeter, Load Impact	Blazemeter, Load Impact
Monitoring	Alert Notification, Activity Tracker, New Relic, Pager Duty, Cloud Monitoring	New Relic	New Relic, Dynatrace
Dynamic Security Tests	App Scan		

What about ICDDE on IaaS?

IaaS, in comparison to PaaS, provides infrastructure only. The provider is just responsible for hardware, virtual servers, networks, storage associated with the applications. The management of middleware, runtimes, and operating system is not available as in PaaS. So how is the development done on IaaS? The answer lies in setting up an own platform or ICDDE on infrastructure provided by IaaS. Private ICDDE, as we may call it, provides the same features as a public ICDDE. However, for private ICDDE, it is essential to build Policy Controls and Governance around the platform use.

Example of a private ICDDE on IaaS:

DevOps phase	Redhat Openshift
PaaS	OpenShift
Source Code Repository	GitHub, GitLab
Organize and Plan	Any external third party, JIRA being most popular today
Build, Continuous Integration, & Deployment	Runtimes, Jenkins
Logging	Elasticsearch, Kibana
Performance Tests	Blazemeter, Load Impact
Monitoring	Prometheus
Dynamic Security Tests	App Scan

6.2 Need for a Lab

Experimenting is one of the important aspects of design thinking that we discussed earlier. We also stated that using the latest technology, researching and learning is also a continuous process of product innovation. For that purpose, the lab environment is also an important part of product development.

Technologies today have a far smaller shelf life, and for every business requirement, there is a multitude of technologies. New technology adoption requires not only the decision made on the viability but also the path to adopting it. It requires a deep understanding of the technology which cannot be attained only through passive means, i.e., reading the documentation, participating in a forum, or watching videos. Labs bring in an agile approach in MVP and POC phases.

Experiments in the lab will ensure that the new technologies are not only learned but are experienced as well. Through these experiments, the labs become the focal point of making technology advances and thus help attain and maintain the technology edge. A lab provides a playing field to brilliant developers to hone up their skills and also develop deep thinking attitude on theories and concepts by inculcating a sense of deep learning as they get their hands dirty and make mistakes.

Smart and strategic organizations always invest in R&D through labs, and we have ample success stories through the big technology organizations of the world today to prove that.

6.3 Sprint Management

Epic, Story and story points

User stories describe in simple language the outline of the desired outcome. A user story is an end goal, not a feature, expressed from the software user's perspective. Unlike the requirement gathering by a business analyst in typical enterprise application development, stories keep the focus on the user, enable collaboration, and drive the creation of solutions. A user story must include three fundamental elements- persona, need, and purpose for the desired outcome.

A story point is an estimated measure of the degree of complexity of implementing a user story, counted as a measure of effort required to implement it. The difficulty could be related to complexities, risks, and efforts involved. A story point is a relative value designated to each story. A story that is assigned two story points (or 20 story points) should be twice as much as a story that is assigned one story point (or 10 story points). It should also be two-thirds of a story that is estimated 3 story points (or 30 story points). Since the story point is a relative number, you can use 1,2, 3... or 10, 20, 30....and for that purpose; it cannot be compared with the story point of another project.

Epics are requirements that increase user engagement with the application. These generally span across multiple sprints. These are further broken into stories. Each epic could be because of one or more features that may be required, need for architectural improvement, supporting the new user interface, application engineering, supporting integrations with external systems, or supporting a mobile app.

Work to plan vs. plan to work

A sprint is a short, set period to deliver a set of stories into a finished product. Sprints make work to be delivered more realizable, allowing teams to deliver work faster and with better quality and more frequently, and give more flexibility to adapt to change. As against the "plan to work" in a typical enterprise application development where the time of delivery is adjusted, and requirements are fixed, the sprint approach is "work to plan" where the time of delivery is fixed and user stories that can be delivered in that time frame are adjusted.

6.3.1 Sprint management lifecycle

Sprint Planning

Sprint Planning establishes deliverables in a sprint and work that will be required to achieve those. Sprint planning is done in collaboration with the full scrum team that includes the product owner and development team. Sprint is kicked off only after planning. In the planning session, the product manager describes the goal of the sprint and what backlog items contribute to that goal. The development team tells how they can or cannot deliver that goal, what inputs they require, and told that what output will be considered as a complete delivery.

Sprint ceremonies

Regular meetings are called as sprint ceremonies to emphasize that they should be religiously conducted and followed with devotion. Although sprint planning can also be deemed as the ceremony but specifically after kick-off, the ceremonies include:

1. Daily stand-up to quickly inform everyone of what is going on across the team. It, not a detailed status meeting. In the daily stand-up, each team member informs everyone else about what did he complete yesterday, what will he work on today, and what is the barrier, if any.

2. Iteration review to showcase or demonstrate the work of the team. Iteration reviews can be casual or conducted in a more formal meeting structure. Iteration review provides an opportunity to celebrate their accomplishments, demonstrate work finished within the iteration, and get immediate feedback from project stakeholders. An important criterion of iteration review is that the work should be fully evident and meet the quality standards to be considered complete and ready to showcase in the review.
3. Retrospectives reviews are meant for the team to understand what worked well-and what went wrong. Retrospectives are not merely complaints sessions, but trigger action for corrections. Retrospective ceremonies are critical for continuous improvement.
4. Sprint reviews are meant to review the work completed and identify the backlog items resulting from the sprint.

Backlog Management

Product Backlog is a real “to-do “list for developers. It includes the stories for bug fixes also. Backlog management is the control process to adds, adjusts, grooms, and prioritizes backlog items within the sprint and roadmap to make sure the delivered product continues to provide the highest possible value to the customers. The product owner manages the backlog. The backlog is built from product roadmap and user stories. A roadmap usually consists of several epics, and each epic will have several user stories. Once the product backlog is built, it is the responsibility of a product owner to maintain it to keep pace with the delivery plan regularly. Product owners should review the backlog and customer feedback from the last iteration every time before an iteration is planned in order to ensure a correct prioritization of the features planned to be covered in a sprint. Keeping the backlog healthy by regular review and maintenance is referred to as backlog grooming and one of the most important parts of backlog management.

The backlog makes the relationship collaborative between the product owner and the product development team. The product owner can dynamically re-prioritize work in the backlog at any time due to customer feedback, refinement of requirements, or new requirements. However, when the sprint is started, the product managers should keep the changes to the sprint scope to a minimum as those would disrupt the development team and would affect the focus, flow, and possibly the team morale.

6.4 Role of Quality Assurance

Quality Assurance (QA) includes the set of policies, procedures, practices, methodologies, frameworks, and organizational structures designed to provide reasonable assurance that quality objectives will be achieved and that the bugs in the code will be prevented. It is the system that comprises of controls, processes, tools, and methods that assure that the quality standards of the software product are achieved if practiced as prescribed. Like security controls, it keeps on identifying and addressing the potential causes of defects.

Essentials for QA

It is important to manage Quality Assurance with a plan of how it will be carried out. The plan should consider which tools and activities are best for the job and also the level of team skills. There should be quality gates that should be set to evaluate the performance based on collected data on different quality gates. The Quality Assurance team should maintain good relations with other teams involved in the project development. QA team should also run educational programs within the DevOps organization on QA activities and objectives which are applicable for the software being developed.

QA vs. Testing

Testing is the set of activities taken up to detect bugs in the software so that they are fixed. The tests are run by a series of repeated and also different inspections. Fixes follow each run of testing or inspection. After the fixes have been done, another review is done to detect whether the bugs still exist or new ones have got introduced. This cycle continues until the time inspections reveal zero bugs. Testing intends to make the software defect-free, in turn, helping to make it run the way it was designed as. Having a defect-free product helps realize the objective that the product meets the expectations.

However, QA prevents defects by making sure that the processes that manage and create the deliverables work to avoid defects. A process that fails to detect a bug needs to be checked and re-engineered by QA.

Quality Assurance, by itself, does not guarantee that there will be no defects in the system. It is the testing that ensures the existence of defects in the system. While testing happens at each stage of development, QA encompasses all the DevOps stages.

In the Cloud Native world, since the goals are to make and release the software as fast as possible, the software testing approach is also different. The goal is to test smarter rather than putting up a lot of effort and yet targeting the delivery of a high-quality product. For this, the developers and testers have to achieve a high level of collaboration, which has to be ongoing, starting the development stage itself. It decreases the feedback time and helps maintain a bug-free code. Testing is not just done by the testers alone; it is the developers also who perform the testing.

Both QA and Testing are required to deliver a successful product. They are used together to identify the processes that lead to defects and identify the bugs in the system.

6.5 Distractions

A lot of times, there are changes required to be made in the components of your product. There may be many reasons for looking to make this change; however, we emphatically prescribe that only the following purposes should drive this change:

1. a better technology as a replacement
2. sunset of existing technology or its support
3. poor support on existing technology
4. porting on another cloud requires existing technology change
5. building a new feature requires current technology change
6. commercial reasons that promise a better ROI

Reasons other than above should surely be rejected as they

are only leading to distractions. The developer time is precious, and hence their efforts should be judiciously spent. Switching to new technology should be carefully adopted because it has implications that may not be known without a detailed analysis of factors like learning/retraining of the staff, migration efforts from existing technology, the complexity of migration, and time and delay in time to market.

6.6 Composing/Assembling a Product

Considering that a Cloud Native application architecture is microservice and API based, it is easy to conceptualize that a product can be composed and assembled on a platform with multiple microservices. It is a de facto understanding is that a microservice is a black box and can be consumed using an API. The consumer has no control over the functionality of microservices. We want to introduce an idea of the configuration ability of a microservice. Many business applications require customer engagement and workflow automation and, therefore, configurable policies. Let us illustrate with an example of approval functionality. In many business scenarios, approval is an integral part of many applications. In order to envisage approval function as a microservice and use with APIs, it will require a microservice with configurable approval policy or many microservices for each one prescribed for a specific approval policy, and that would be non-viable. If microservices functionality can be configured, then it would be straightforward to realize the concept of composing a product. In our product development, we brought in the concept of Class A and Class B microservices and differentiated as follows:

Class A Microservice	Class B Microservice
Consumable by APIs	Consumable by APIs
Rich features & functionalities	Limited but focused function
Allow consumer/composer to configure and admin features and functions	Consume only, no configuration allowed
Heavyweight and can be conceptually treated as a standalone application	Lightweight, published on the Internet and can be embedded in the platform
Example- Approval Engine, Notification engine	Example - GoogleMaps, AccuWeather

The following diagram illustrates the comparison between the building and composing an application.

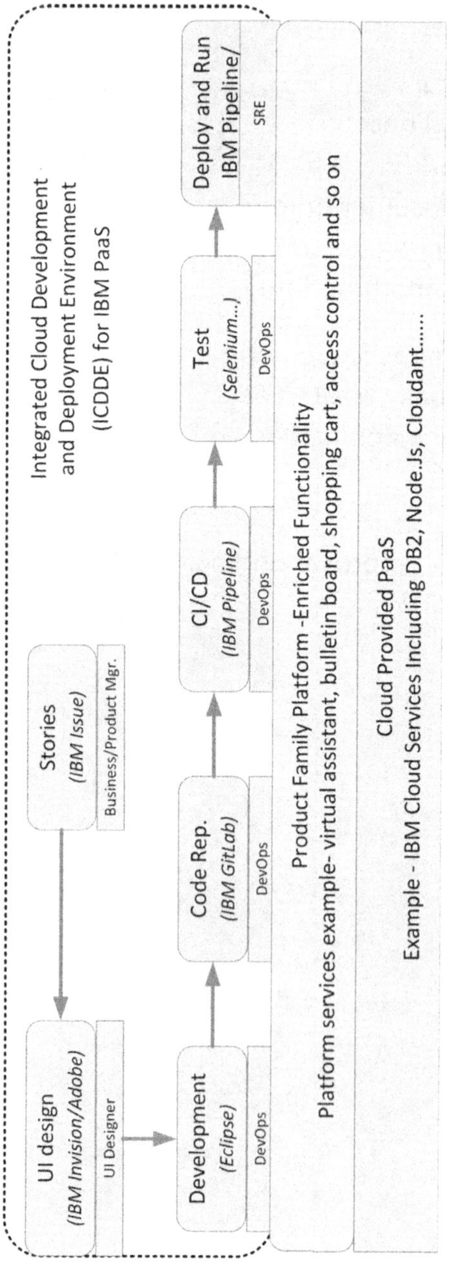

Figure 24: Building CN application- IBM PaaS Example

For building, you do a substantial amount of coding while reusing the standard platform services for the product family.

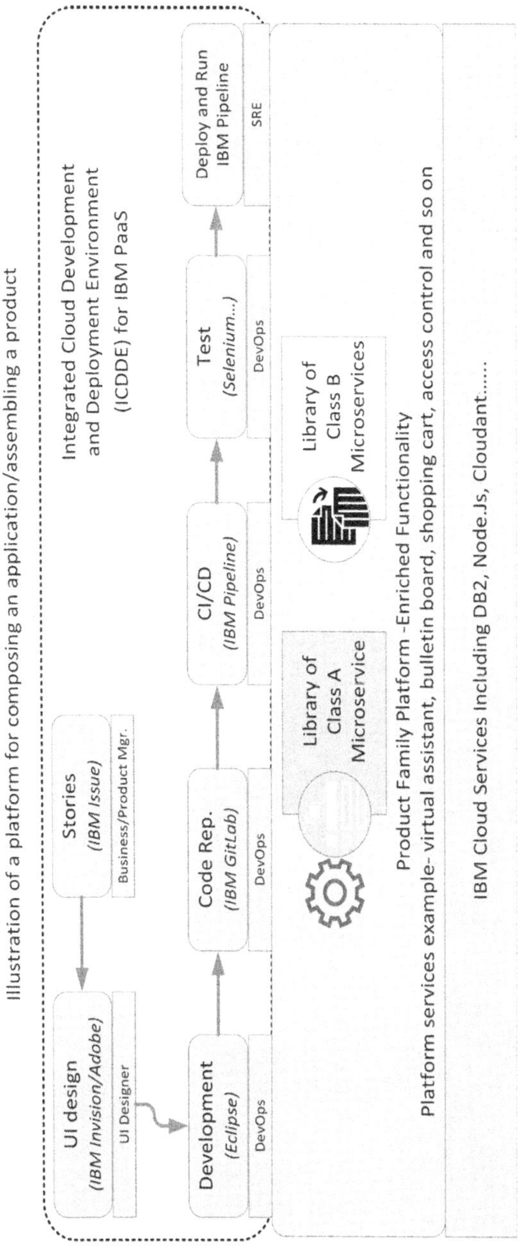

Figure 25: Composing CN Application- IBM PaaS example

Composing a Cloud Native product on a platform is the first step towards a low code/no-code approach in the Cloud Native world.

7 RUNNING PRODUCT IN SAAS MODEL

SaaS is a method of delivering software through a subscription, rather than being bought and installed on individual computers. The software is accessed online as a business service running on a cloud, and enterprises can access it for its users through license subscriptions on a pay-as-you-go model. In this mode, the service provider undertakes several responsibilities from that a customer would have otherwise taken, and most prominent among them is hosting and management of infrastructure and application upgrades. In other words, apart from the build, most of the run also comes in the scope of the product owner.

7.1 The business substance is the codebase

Each codebase is a high-value IP and revenue-producing asset. Every product company is solely valued for what software product it has and the value of IP within it. Buyers pay for that IP as a license fee. Most of the enterprises are now realizing the importance of owning IP and developing their business applications as products. As such, the technology has become the core of every business, and codes are virtually running every business; the product development approach works well. I heard one of the financial industry CEO claiming themselves as the technology company that happens to be in the financial business.

Code lifecycle management is, therefore, central to the business and keeping the business value. Regardless of the offering model and charging model, the operations revolve around the codebase.

Codebase, Instance and customer domain

In the earlier section, we have explained the codebase. One codebase can have multiple instances deployed, and each instance would have one customer (dedicated) or more customers. In the context of an enterprise, you can think of a department or a business unit, or a geographical location could be a customer. If the product is designed for multitenancy, one instance can have domain separated customers.

The application in the SaaS delivery model is a cloud service that is made operational for a customer before it is ready for use. A SaaS application offers a standard feature set that allows some level of configuration for each customer but does not allow any customization. The deployment times are considered smaller than traditional software because the SaaS application comes pre-packaged with features that a client enterprise needs. It is the provider's responsibility to ensure that backups are taken, the application is scalable, the application remains available, and upgrades happen as per the agreements it has with the application customers who are SaaS subscribers. These are considered to be done faster and automated without any risk of breaking any feature in usage. In all of this, maintaining the integrity and having a limited number of application codebases are the key factors to ensure.

SaaS enables clients to subscribe to the services that it needs and for the required number of users. In its real sense, there should typically be no customization or code change done for any customer, and it should only allow some level of configuration on a standard feature set for a customer. However, there are times when code changes are necessitated because of requirements to meet the customer needs even through customizations, or application's feature set immature to abstract a code change from a configuration change that is required by the customer. And this is where the providers get challenged in maintaining the SaaS service. To run the application in SaaS mode and effective and efficient services are made available from a SaaS application, providers should ensure the following:

1. Maintain limited application versions across all instances - A provider cannot have limitless versions of the same application. All major SaaS providers limit the count to three. It means that there should be limits on the time customers can be given leverage on agreeing to the upgrades.

2. Analyze the feasibility - A customer who has spent years with the same system is reluctant to change because the current application is time tested. Such customers need to be on-boarded on a SaaS service after a careful analysis of their requirements being met by the SaaS service. Only after the study finds onboarding to be affirmative, the onboarding should happen.

3. Right onboarding strategy - For large customers, on-boarding should happen in a staggered way based on

the number of users. A big bang approach may result in the SaaS service being not used at all or the application becoming a bespoke application for the customer.

4. Agree on service terms - Service terms on availability, upgrades, and performance are agreed upon and form the basis for the providers to provide the capacity.

5. Correct integration approach - Integrations in the cloud era are different from traditional integrations. The volume of data has grown which requires scalable integrations, the type of data has changed from a row and column combination to being less structured which requires a late-binding approach, data now traverses datacenter into cloud which needs data to be collected where it resides, and identity of access has become complicated which requires changed integration technologies and methodologies. Integrations are typical of each client, and care should be taken to as much abstract the application from the integration as possible.

6. Setting up domain boundaries - A multi-tenant application instance needs to maintain a logical separation of data between various tenants it holds. It can either be done through the logical separation of data in the same data store or a physical separation through having different data stores.

7. Right-sizing - Sizing of the resources should be dependent on the required data and transaction volumes considering the business requirements of each customer. One size cannot fit all.

7.2 Deployment Technology and Architecture

The liberation of the deployment technology with the development technology is among the technical benefits of the Cloud Native world. In the legacy client-server world, a deployment architecture maps the logical architecture to a physical environment which consists of the computing nodes, processors, memory, storage, and its devices, and other hardware and network pieces required. In the Cloud Native world, it would be mapping to cloud services and resources.

Deployment Model

There are four deployment models, as described below. The choice is dependent upon the business needs. All these are offered by all major cloud service providers and have similar benefits, performance, and reliability.

1. Private onsite - Computing resources are exclusive for an enterprise and are hosted in the enterprise datacenter. Other features are:
   a. It is a costlier model even if the hardware is non-allocated in the enterprise DC as there is a software cost involved.
   b. A fixed amount of infrastructure resources are available as per the sizing is done for anticipated workloads and costs.
   c. Security measures as considered appropriate and applicable for in house resources can be applied.

It is more suitable for business-critical and security-sensitive applications and is mostly used by government agencies and financial institutions.

2. Private outsourced - Computing resources are exclusive for

an enterprise and are hosted in a cloud service or a third-party vendor's datacenter. Other features are:

a. It is less costly than onsite options as the resources are provisioned and managed by the provider. There are additional costs related to SLA support from the vendor and the secured connections that may have to be built between the enterprise data center to the outsourced

d. private cloud.

There is flexibility in the number of resources but are

c. governed by SLAs with a third party.

Security measures as considered appropriate and applicable for in house resources can be applied but on third party datacenter. Plus, the connections that may have to be built between the enterprise data center to the outsourced private cloud are to be made secure.

It is more suitable for applications that are not mission-critical and are not as much security sensitive but either require isolation from the public traffic or have exceptional performance and availability considerations not available through shared resources. It is mostly used by enterprises requiring more control of the infrastructure environment.

3. Public - Cloud resources are owned and managed by the services provider. Infrastructure resources - hardware, storage, and network devices are shared with other enterprises. Other features are:
   a. There are lower costs as compared to private models.
   b. There is no restriction on the number of resources that can be used.
   c. There is limited control over security measures as compared to the above options.

It is mostly used for applications that require access to a large volume of data, are not mission-critical, and there is no security sensitivity.

4. Hybrid - A mix of both private (onsite or third party) and public, it is used to provide an option to move data and applications between private and public clouds. There is greater flexibility in deciding upon the deployment options. One basis could be the type of application - enterprises can decide upon hosting on the private or public clouds. The other basis could be cloud bursting - when an application utilization of resources spikes in the private cloud, it starts tapping the resources from the public cloud.

Hosting considerations

When it is about hosting the applications on a cloud, there are four available choices - container, virtual machine, serverless computing, or a bare metal server. The first three choices of cloud computing are virtual choices running on physical hardware, which is shared amongst multiple clients. However, the bare metal server is the physical server that is hosted on the cloud and is dedicated to a client.

While we have explained containers in the "Container" section, let us look at what serverless computing is. Serverless computing is a method of utilizing compute services on an as-used basis. There is no server, and whenever the application is accessed, it triggers events on a serverless platform. It can be an excellent solution to avoid paying for idle time and letting the platform scale as needed. Serverless computing still requires virtual servers for deploying the application, but those are in an "inactive" state until the event to access them is triggered. There is no infrastructure provisioning required to be done beforehand.

We will now mention the hosting considerations for the first three choices. As far as the fourth choice, which is the bare metal server, is concerned, those are the same as for a server hosted in the enterprise DC.

1. Portability
   a. Containers offer more flexibility than a VM in terms of porting as faster deployment is possible through small startup times. It takes a few seconds to start versus minutes for a virtual machine. Therefore, the portability of containers is better.
   b. Serverless computing offers a lesser level of flexibility in portability as provided by containers as there is vendor lock-in.

2. Image maintenance
   a. Maintenance of container image is easier than of a VM as the image is smaller because it just contains what is required to run the application rather than the whole virtual environment.
   b. An IT team is required to create a VM image, whereas a developer can create a container image.

3. Security
   a. Deployment on the container is less secure than on a VM as it runs as a process isolated from other processes running on top of the same host OS.
   b. Deployment on serverless computing is as secure as it is for the container.

4. Consistency
   a. The operating environment is consistent between various environments of an application deployed on containers.
   b. The operating environment for the deployed application cannot be changed without creating a new container.
   c. The operating environment is consistent between various environments of an application deployed on serverless computing.

5. Provisioning
   a. Faster provisioning time for containers as the control gates for a container is far simpler than for a virtual machine.
   b. Provisioning for serverless computing is event-based and is on demand.

6. Lifetime
   a. Containers have a smaller lifetime. Every application deployment results in the replacement of an existing container with a new container.
   b. Serverless computing goes inactive after the action is taken on the event.

7. Resource Sharing
   a. A container generally hosts one application, whereas a VM hosts multiple ones.
   b. Serverless computing comes into action only upon the response to an event.

8. Workload Suitability
   a. For containers:
      i. number of apps running on a server needs to be maximized

ii. multiple instances of a single application running on the same operating environment
iii. quick starts
iv. the application should run on any underlying infrastructure

b. For virtual machines:
   i. multiple operating systems
   ii. multiple apps on a single server
   iii. the app requires all the resources and functionalities of an OS
   iv. full isolation and security is required

c. For serverless computing:
   i. The server is active only when running
   ii. Not for long-running apps
   iii. Task latency is tolerable
   iv. Lesser control on memory or compute resources
   v. Not suitable for large and complex apps

Please note the finer differences between microservice computing and serverless computing. Microservices that are a part of long-running apps are not suitable to be hosted as serverless applications. The larger difference is the commercial model between the running container and running serverless compute.

7.3 Functional Teams in Operating Model

The functional team structure is one of the pillars of the operating model of the Cloud Native application in the SaaS model. A codebase can be deployed in a cloud foundry container (garden container) or a docker container. If you choose not to use the CF container, then there is an additional responsibility for image management. This responsibility can be entrusted to SRE or can be retained with the DevOps team who maintains the codebase.

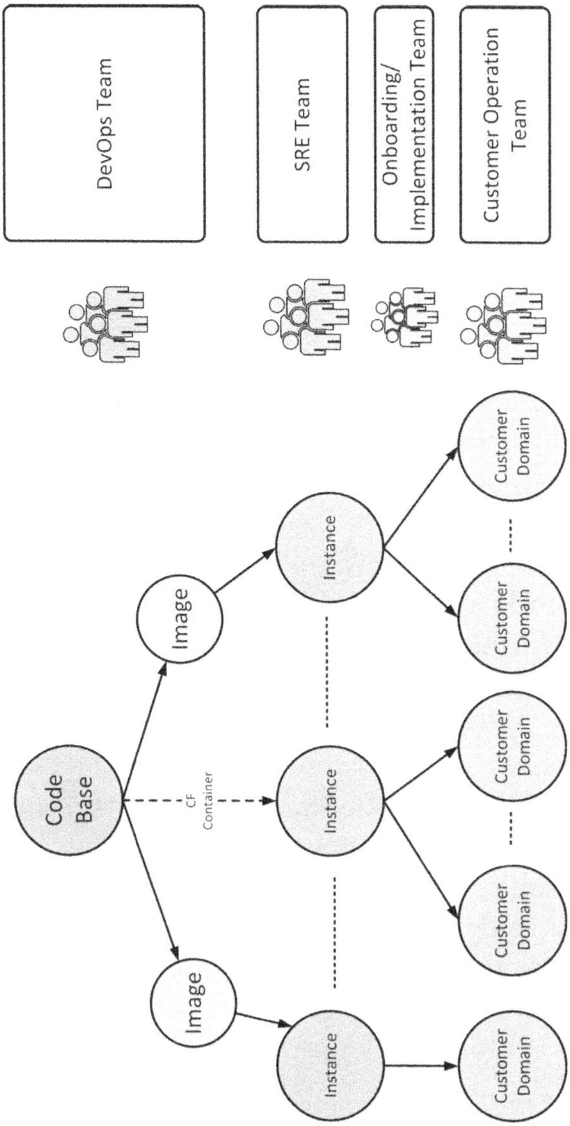

Figure 26: Functional Teams for SaaS Operations

We prefer to entrust the responsibility of image management to DevOps team for the following reasons:

a. The image can be treated as an extended codebase and integrity can be mainlined by a common set of principles
b. Checks on image suitability and utility may show issues with the code or its dependencies. These would have to be fixed at the code level. DevOps team is responsible for the maintenance of codebase will be fixing those issues.
c. Verifying the integrity and suitability of the image will be the responsibility of the SRE team.

DevOps Team

We have written adequately about the agile and DevOps model in the earlier section. In the context of SaaS operation model and the functional team structure, the roles and responsibilities of the DevOps team include-

Manage the utility and warrant of the code: By utility, we mean that the code is fit for the purpose, and by warranty, we mean it is fit for use. DevOps team is the creator and the owner of the code, so all their responsibilities revolve around the codebase. Typical utility attributes are features, functions, and alignment to the business requirements of the purpose for which it was written. The warranty attribute of the code is free of defect and usability related matter that includes nonfunctional requirement compliance and user experience attributes as well. Utility and warranty of the code are different than the utility and warranty of the instance. But it would be the responsibility of the DevOps team to design and build the instrumentations for monitoring.

Continually enrich, enhance, and expand the code based on

the product roadmap: Product has a vision and corresponding roadmap, so the development and DevOps work do not end at the release. Software Product life span is long and may run for decades also. So long as the product is in the market and is supported, the DevOps role will continue to add the code.

Focus on how to build what code, and this includes product architect & design. The architecture and design work does not end with the release of MVP. It continues as the roadmap progresses, although the level of the design requirement will increase, and the coding efforts will increase with time. The roadmap may also require some architectural adjustments.

Team composition - In terms of the skillset, the DevOps team should have the skills of Cloud Native Architect (CNA), Cloud Native Developer (CND), Data Engineer, Integration Engineer, GUI Developers, and Testers.

Squads in DevOps

Squads are small teams in your DevOps organization that deliver upon a specific capability. They do it independently as a team and collaborate with other squads. The reason to have various squads is to let each squad have the freedom to decide how to build a specific capability and how to work together building it. The squad is autonomous as it consists of members of diverse backgrounds. The basis of deciding upon a squad composition is the capability goal that the squad is targeted to deliver. The squad works as a cohesive unit of folks who work together to achieve the assigned goal. The squad approach is, therefore, suitable for large products that require large teams.

Site Reliability Engineer (SRE)

SRE concept was introduced mastered by Google. A site is what produces the service and is exposed to the users via a URL. A lot of books are published on site reliability engineering. We want to mention this team role in the context of our operating model.

Manage the utility and warranty of the instance: Similar to the utility and warranty of application code; we need the utility and warranty of the instance. By utility, we mean that the instance is performing, and by warranty, we mean that the instance is available. In other words, all the measurements and parameters of availability and performance are for application, and it is the prime responsibility of SRE. Therefore, SREs will be monitoring the availability and the performance and mitigating the risks proactively and reactively.

The team will deploy and monitor instances use the instrumentation build by DevOps and native cloud services for monitoring. Third-party tools can be used.

Continually enhance the instance reliability and performance:

- Focus on how to run on what platform (Own deployment Architecture)
- Team composition-PRE, SRE, Data Engineer, Integration Engineer

Customer Ops

Customer Ops is a function related to the operation of the layer above code that includes the configuration and set up of the SaaS application and if allowed the required customization for the specific customer. This function does the Customer support for application operation and the team composition App admin and customer-specific data management.

Customer operations are responsible for operating the application on behalf of a customer for the specific roles in the app. It is done to fulfill specific tasks in the application which are associated with the function concerned. Responsibilities include but are not limited to, the following:

- Maintenance of the master data
- Taking periodic reports from the system
- Participation in service reviews
- Review of the system performance
- Testing new features related to the tasks responsible for
- Provide feedback on new features
- Provide inputs on new feature demand
- Educate other users for the tasks responsible for
- Provide information on repetitive work that can be automated, and be a stakeholder in the building of such automation by the DevOps team
- Be a stakeholder in setting up of integrations around the tasks responsible for

Platform Reliability Engineer (PRE)

Although it is convenient to use the development platform and the environment from the cloud provider, there may be scenarios where you may like to build your platform on-premise or on the cloud.

Platform Reliability Engineers are responsible for supporting and maintaining a platform for the developers. The platform is a custom platform, e.g., OpenShift platform. The custom platforms allow running assembling the platform with custom tools and cloud services and can handle hybrid deployments. The PRE team assists in building and running the custom platforms for the development team. PRE for the platforms utilized from a cloud services provider does not manage the platform but can serve as an extended development team in enhancing the adoption of the services the platform has to offer.

8 PRODUCT MAINTENANCE

Product Maintenance is required to keep the product defect and vulnerability free and to improve upon its functioning, robustness, and performance. Software complexity is growing as it seeks to address more and more business complexities. With complexity, interdependencies are increasing, which in turn contributes to increased complexity. Code changes happening so frequently also add to the complexity as developers are desperate to meet new demands in as little time as possible and, in turn, tend up pushing the codebase itself into a dire state even though maintaining high quality is assumed to be part of a developer's job.

The maintenance aspects that are associated with your product need to be targeted regularly, which is guided by the rate of changes in the code as well as upon a change in a dependent external component. Let us look at the maintenance related changes that can come about in a product and the things that need to be kept into consideration while performing these:

Feature Additions

An evolving product requires new features to be added from time to time. With new features, the following things need to be taken care of:

1. No dead code: A feature addition should not end up adding dead code pieces.
2. Simple code: Use of language constructs for easy readability and understanding
3. Avoid code creeps: Care should be taken to reuse the existing code to the extent possible. With advances in languages, component-based development is possible, and identifying a current component to reuse should be the first step.
4. Preserve interdependencies - Cloud Native development requires developers to learn to develop to contract. At no point, these contracts should get broken and break the component interdependencies.

Refactoring

Existing code would require to be refactored because of either feature drops, or finding better ways to meet the same requirement, or to fix bugs or meet new needs of performance or fixing of new or existing security vulnerabilities. The considerations are the same as mentioned before for Feature Additions.

External Components

A lot more development today is dependent on components developed by third parties. Following are the considerations related to external dependencies when those are added or upgraded:

1. Future maintenance - The components should remain maintained at all times by their respective providers.
2. License compliance - Upgrades may result in license compliance issues for components that today are license-free.
3. Security vulnerabilities - Adding a new component or upgrading an existing component should not add security vulnerabilities.
4. Performance Implications - Performance should not be negatively impacted.
5. New bugs - The introduction of new bugs should not happen.
6. Preserve interdependencies - The existing contracts should get broken and break the component interdependencies.
7. Remain current - All packages should be upgraded to newer versions when those are available.
8. If the application is impacted negatively, changing the code to adapt to the change rather than looking to change the component or remaining with the old versioned component is a better option in terms of costs and risks associated.

Cloud Platform Services

Cloud Native applications utilize a lot of services available on the cloud, e.g., database, ci/cd, auto-scaling, infrastructure, monitoring, etc. The considerations are the same as mentioned before for External Components.

9 ANNEXURE: SPECIALIZED CLOUD - IPAAS

Integration technology in Cloud Native Era

No application can be standalone in any enterprise, and integration is imperative for Cloud Native app development also. Integration is an essential part of every application. In the contemporary business world of cloud and mobile, connect everything, everywhere from anywhere, is an essential need and demand of the users and the businesses. That brings the importance of the integration platform, the new generation of integration technology.

iPaaS vs ESB

Bus architecture originated from the hardware where a bus is a group of wires that connects different components of the computer. It is used for transmitting data, control signals, and memory addresses from one component to another. Every computer manufacturer has its proprietary bust architecture. In the personal computer industry, ISA Bus became the universal standard. However, MCA (Micro Channel Architecture) was also quite popular but proprietary. Likewise, for software and application integrations, an Enterprise Service Bus (ESB) is fundamentally an architecture. It is a set of protocols and generic technical standards for integrating numorous applications over a bus-like infrastructure. ESB provides several functionalities namely Invocation, Routing, Mediation, Messaging, Process choreography, Service orchestration, Complex event processing, Agnosticism, Protocol Conversion, Validation, Governance, Enrichment, Abstraction, Transformation, Commodity Services, Audit and logging for 'any to any" application interaction and management of entire interaction.

ESB architectures are much more sophisticated. They also need to be scalable and available and performance-driven. Offering ESB architecture in the cloud with a commercial model of pay by use is iPaaS. (Integration Platform as a Service). It could have been very well termed as ESB in the cloud, but that would still carry the name ESB, and that is old. To sell in the market, you need something new. That is how iPaaS appeared as the buzzword.

The analogy of airport hub with ESB

Long before the introduction of ESB architecture in software technology, the Airline industry implemented the concept of a service bus for passenger traffic and baggage exchange at airport hub locations with fantastic maturity.

Think of an aircraft as an application and airport gate as the application port. Think of passengers as the data packet. Some passengers need to be transferred to other aircraft at another gate. It requires the routing of the passenger. There will be a defined window of transfer, and time out will result in rerouting to another flight in addition to deterioration in the service. The new aircraft will have different seating configurations, so seat numbers need to be transformed.

Depending upon the domestic transfer or international transfer, the routing and transformation protocol will be different. The passenger needs to be informed all the time, and so the target gate attendant. Airport security and passenger security need to be maintained, and prevention of unauthorized access or wrong passenger boarding is mandatory. It could be across the different carriers. Depending upon the connection time, the passenger may need additional services like food and restroom.

Passengers can also add additional carry-on baggage (duty-free purchase) that may need additional verifications. For international transfer, extra security and control protocols like passport and visa entitlement may be required. Events like weather or connecting flight schedules need to be processed. In the nutshell, all the functionalities of ESB namely Invocation, Routing, Mediation, Messaging, Process choreography, Service orchestration, Complex event processing, Agnosticism, Protocol Conversion, Validation, Governance, Enrichment, Abstraction, Transformation, Commodity Services, Audit and logging for 'any to any" airline traffic exchange are applicable. What more complex is the requirement that baggage should also be transferred with the same passenger and airlines have been doing it successfully with commendable accuracy and within SLA. On the contrary, in ESB architecture, the "linked data packet" transfer is not that easy. I would not hesitate to say the ESB has learned from the airline hub idea and have learned more about real business architecture.

The difference between data and application integration

Data integration is the merging of data from different data sources into a combined view that is meaningful and valuable to the users. Data integration achieves four objectives through the combined view - standardization of combined data, providing for portability of combined data, elimination of redundancy, and ensuring the quality of data.

Application integration, on the other hand, links two applications. It is very much a real-time sharing of information between online transaction processing systems. It requires an enterprise application integration (EAI) middleware for quick and easy communication between the applications. Application integration often actively manages the flow of information between applications, usually via an application programming interface (API) in real-time between two or more applications upon an event happening in one application. It can become even more complicated when integrating on-premises legacy systems with newer, cloud-based services. Different types of integration require different platforms and methodologies. While data integration combines data sets from multiple sources, application integration transforms and transports data from one application to another. Application integration also means that integration mechanism has to not only take care of replicating the data, which is unstructured but also take care of bursts, late binding, and meeting the security and access requirements of each application it is required to integrate.

9.1 Data Integration Patterns

Migration

Migration is the process of moving or replicating a dataset from one system to the other. It involves a source system where the data originally resides before the process execution, at least one criterion which determines the data to be migrated, a transformation that changes the format of data, a destination system where the data will be inserted, and finally, the confirmation of successful movement.

Migrations occur when you are moving from one system to another, moving from one system instance to another or a newer instance of the same system, spinning up a new system instance that extends the current infrastructure, backing up a dataset, adding nodes to database clusters, replacing database hardware, consolidating systems, moving to cloud, and many more.

Migrations are an essential aspect of all data systems and are used extensively in any organization. Enterprises invest a lot of time and effort in creating and maintaining data, and migration is vital to keep that data-agnostic from the tools that we use to create it, view it, and manage it. Data is the digital asset, and without migration, an enterprise may lose it.

Aggregation

Data aggregation is the process of receiving data from multiple systems and inserting them into one system. The aggregation is very beneficial to extract and process data from multiple systems in one united application. It ensures that data being consolidated is up to date at the time required, is owned in the source system, and can be aggregated or merged to produce the consolidated dataset required.

The aggregation pattern helps to create orchestration APIs to "modernize" legacy systems, especially when you are creating an API that queries data from various sources and then processes it into a response with aggregated data. A use case is for creating reports or dashboards which provide a single view on data pulled from multiple systems.

Broadcast

Broadcast is moving of data from a single source system to multiple destination systems on an ongoing basis in real-time or near real-time whenever there is a change in data in the source system.

The broadcast pattern moves the data in one direction, from the source to the destination, and happens on a per transaction basis. It means it does not execute the logic of the destination system for all data; instead, it runs the logic only for the data that has recently changed.

The broadcast is most appropriate when the destination system needs to know the data as soon as it is captured in the source system, and that data needs to flow automatically; however, the source system need not know what happens to the data in the destination system.

Bi-directional Sync

Bi-directional sync combines two datasets in two systems to make them be seen as one dataset while continuing to exist as two different datasets. The need is to have separate systems for accomplishing different functions and still fulfill the need for a combined dataset. Bidirectional sync is useful when you have two or more independent dataset representations in use.

Data Correlation

The correlation data integration is a bi-directional data sync of the intersection of two data sets if that data item occurs in both systems naturally. It is similar to how the bi-directional pattern synchronizes the union of the scoped datasets. Items

stored in both systems may have been created in each of those systems, e.g., two service desk personnel entering the same call in two systems. Items may have been brought in as part of an integration. The correlation pattern will agnostically synchronize items as long as they are found in both systems rather than caring about the origin.
The correlation data integration pattern is appropriate in cases where there are two systems to share data if there is a record representing the same item in both. Having extra data here is considered to be more costly than beneficial because it allows you to keep out the "unnecessary" data.

Transformation

It is the process of converting data types and format of the data to be migrated from one of the source systems to the one which is accepted by the destination system. An example could be the conversion of XML data into a CSV file that is accepted by the destination system. Apart from type and format, the transformation could also cover the removal of duplicates, enrichment of data by looking up data in reference data sources.

9.2 Application Integration Patterns

With the popularity of SaaS-based applications, application integration has become far more complex and, therefore, specialized than it was ever before. Hybrid architectures, unstructured data sources, need to have data reflected in a real-time, massive influx of data, sophisticated transformations, are few of the challenges posed. It is not possible in the cloud world to have a single application, which is all by itself or stand-alone. The cloud-based applications are far more connected to other applications than before. The application integration patterns guide integration designers to help streamline the processes and flows of integration between two applications. Let us look briefly at one of the published materials on the application integration patterns:

1. Integration Styles - This specifies how the integration will happen. There is guidance available on the decision factors to decide upon one of the following options:
   a. File transfer which involves data to be replicated being available through files which are shared between the applications
   b. Databases being shared or set common between two applications
   c. Remote procedure invocation by one application on another to pull or push data
   d. Messaging to exchange data as messages.

2. Message Channels - A channel connects two applications and governs how data wrapped in a message is transported. There is guidance available on the decision factors to decide upon one of the following:
   a. One to one or one to many - Could lead to a decision on point to point or publisher-subscriber channels.
   b. Type of data - The kind of data to be exchanged has to be agreed between the two systems. A channel can be used to move data only of one type. If an application is known to transmit two different types of data, it has to utilize two separate channels for the purpose.
   c. Wrong and dead messages- Guidance on what to do with the messages that are undelivered to a destination.
   d. Unavailable channel - Guidance on what happens to the message if the channel is unavailable.
   e. Non-messaging clients - Guidance on the use of adapters for applications that are not connected to the channel.

applications that are not connected to the channel.

f. Communications backbone - Guidance on making the messaging system the centralized bus for all application integration needs.

3. Message Construction - Guidance on intent, form, and content of the message that flows. It also considers the size and scale and speed of message replication.

4. Routing Pattern - Guidance on how to route messages from a source to a destination. It could mean moving between different channels. The destination could be static or dynamic based on rules. If dynamic, the determination of the destination depends on the message content.

5. Transformation Pattern - Guidance on changing the data to format and type that the destination systems can understand. It may require enrichment with the data that the source system cannot supply. It could be a computation or looking up in a reference system.

6. End Point Pattern - Guidance on how an application connects to a messaging system to send and receive messages. It includes setting up the integration layer for the application to create and send the message, how to consume messages including throttling, synchronous or asynchronous acceptance, message assignments or grab, accept all or filter.

7. System Management Patterns - Guidance on tools to manage the messaging ecosystem, which consists of error conditions arising out of bottlenecks and changes in participants. It includes monitoring and analyzing traffic.

10 About the Authors

Rahul Kandhari

Rahul Kandhari is a software developer who has grown to be a software architect and designer over the last 21 years he has spent in the industry. He has worked in various assignments as a software programmer, implementation consultant, architect, and designer.

After being there for over two decades, he finds fascinating that though the developers have been repeatedly told about the criticality of software for the business which means that it has been a fact for a long time, the business itself never considered software as critical until quite recently when cloud nativity started to gain traction. It is this fascination, along with the project to develop two software products, which led him to pursue his learning on cloud nativity. Over the last four years, his focus has been to create software in a way that allows faster, reliable, and constant changes to meet the changing needs of users and product managers while maintaining the principle of an efficient application backed by an effective design as fundamental as ever. In doing so, he has built a software team structure that encourages design and collaborative thinking and instills confidence in the developers of being co-partners in development and being amongst the best.

Rahul holds a Masters in Computer Applications and works for HCL Technologies Limited at Noida, India.

Prafull Verma

Prafull Verma has a bachelor's degree in electronics and communication engineering and has over thirty years of experience in the area of electronic data processing and Information Technology. He started his career in India in electronic data processing systems and later moved to the United States in 1997. In the past thirty years, he has worked on diversified areas in Computer Science and information technologies. Some of his key experience areas are design and implementation of heterogeneous networks, midrange technical support management, end-user service management, and design, and the implementation and management of process-driven ITSM systems.

Prafull has acquired a unique blend of expertise in integrated areas of tools, processes, governance, operations, and technology. He is the author of several methodologies and frameworks for IT service management that include multi-vendor ITIL frameworks, ITSM for cloud computing, and Service Integration.

Prafull's competencies and specializations include merging engineering with service management and outsourcing business management.

Currently, Prafull is working for HCL Technologies Ltd. as Fellow and Chief Architect and responsible for architecting, designing, building the next generation service management products, and delivering services and solutions around the digital service management platforms. He is also serving as a governing board member of The Open Group.

Kalyan Kumar

Kalyan Kumar (KK) is the Chief Technologist for HCL Technologies - ISD and leads all the Global Technology Practices. In his current role, Kalyan is responsible for defining Architecture & Technology Strategy, New Solutions Development & Engineering across all Enterprise Infrastructure, Business Productivity, Unified Communication Collaboration & Enterprise Platform/DevOps Service Lines. Kalyan is also responsible for Business and Service Delivery for Cross-Functional Services for HCL across all service lines globally.

Kalyan is widely acknowledged as an expert and path-breaker on BSM/ITSM & IT Architecture and Cloud Platforms and has developed many IPs for the company in these domains. He is credited with building HCL MTaaS™ Service from scratch, which has a multi-million turnover today and a proprietary benchmark for Global IT Infrastructure Services Delivery. His team is also credited with developing the MyCloudSM platform for Cloud Service Management & MyDevOps, which is a pioneering breakthrough in the Utility Computing and Hybrid Agile Ops Model space. He has been presented with many internal and industry awards for his thought leadership in the IT Management space.

Kalyan also runs the HCL ISD IPDEV Incubator Group, where he is responsible for incubating new services, platforms, and IPs for the company. He is also active in the Digital Systems Integration Roadmap and Solutions Strategy for HCL.

Kalyan has spoken at many prestigious industry platforms and is currently actively engaged in the Partner Advisory Board of CA Technologies, IBM Software, etc.

In his free time, Kalyan likes to jam with his band 'Contraband' as a drummer/percussionist, review Consumer Technology Gadgets, and follow cricket games diligently.

KK can be followed on Twitter @KKLIVE and at Linkedin (http://www.linkedin.com/in/kalyankumar).

From the same Authors

Adapting to Digital Transformation: Design Sensible SLAs for Modern IT

Authored By - Prafull Verma, Mohan Kewalramani, and Kalyan Kumar

Paperback: 188 pages
Publisher: Intelligent IT Operations
Language: English
ISBN-10: 0692889167
ISBN-13: 978-0692889169
Dimensions: 6 x 0.4 x 9 inches

Most enterprises follow the ITIL framework to design, deliver, and operate IT services, which includes developing Service Level Agreements (SLAs). These are, however, associated with technical services, which are not detailed in the guidance provided by ITIL. Although it seems relatively straight forward and easy, the reality is that there are many pitfalls and misconceptions in developing a set of meaningful SLAs that will work seamlessly in a multi-supplier environment. Additionally, the Information Technology landscape is changing rapidly with the emergence of disruptive new technologies underpinned by the Cloud. New business models are evolving in the creation and delivery of IT Services. In the modern world of XaaS - anything and everything-as-a-service, traditional methods and practices are incompatible and need to be adapted, including SLAs, while still supporting the large portions of legacy environments that continue to exist in enterprises. This book provides guidance on the factors to consider when developing SLAs in a traditional as well as modern IT service environment and highlights the common perils to watch out for.

Foundation for XaaS: Service Architecture in the 21st Century Enterprise

Authored by Prafull Verma and Kalyan Kumar

List Price: $12.95
6" x 9" (15.24 x 22.86 cm)
Black & White on White paper
152 pages
Service Integration
ISBN-13: 978-0692688311
(Custom Universal)
ISBN-10: 0692688315
BISAC: Computers / Information Technology

XaaS is a collective term said to stand for several things, including "X as-a-service". Everything (and anything!) as-a-service is a rapidly expanding model not only in cloud service but also in every other industry. It grew from a utility service model and applied to IT and now non-IT services as well. It is the new delivery model and shall warrant a new approach to service management. But before that, it will require a new approach to design and publish a service. Like service management architecture that we discussed in our earlier publication, service architecture is largely an ignored aspect of service design. IT professionals talk more about application architecture than service architecture. This book discusses the sets of service properties that collectively form a service architecture and then also talks about the building blocks of the XaaS service management system.

Foundation of Intelligent IT Operations: CMDB and Service Maps

Authored by Mr. Prafull Verma, Mr. Mohan Kewalramani, and
Mr. Kalyan Kumar

List Price: $15.95
6" x 9" (15.24 x 22.86 cm)
Black & White on White paper
172 pages
Software Asset Management
ISBN-13: 978-0692380925
(Custom Universal)
ISBN-10: 0692380922
BISAC: Computers /
Information Technology

The scale of enterprise IT environments is growing rapidly, and computing resources are deployed in abundance. Consequently, the management of IT operations gets increasingly complex. Service Maps and the CMDB (Configuration Management Database) are key tools to enable an organization to manage the complexity of dependencies and relationships between components intelligently. Theoretically, this sounds reasonable and easily achievable, especially since the concept of a CMDB was introduced in ITIL v2 more than a decade ago, and the assumption is that almost all the organizations that have adopted ITIL would have a CMDB and will be delivering on its intended objectives. The reality is far removed from theory, though.

Designing, implementing, and maintaining a sensible CMDB that is fit for purpose and does not end up being a project set up for failure, requires more than just theoretical knowledge. Additionally, with the rapid adoption of cloud computing, Internet of Things (IoT), and other disruptive technologies in an increasingly complex multi-supplier environment with implementations of "Service Integration and Management (SIAM)", the old school vision of the CMDB needs to be designed with a renewed perspective to keep it relevant to our IT environments today.

This book tries to educate IT generalists with the basics of CMDB and service maps without the need for understanding technology or any specialist tools while trying to guide IT service management professionals to build an intelligent information system that produces the real benefits to support the management of IT services by having a reliable and enriched source of information, that helps in making better, more informed decisions.

Software Asset Management: Understanding and Implementing an Optimal Solution

Authored by Mr. Prafull Verma and Mr. Kalyan Kumar

List Price: $15.95
6" x 9" (15.24 x 22.86 cm)
Black & White on White paper
148 pages
Software Asset Management
ISBN-13: 978-0692324264
(Custom Universal)
ISBN-10: 0692324267
BISAC: Computers /
Information Technology

Software Asset Management (SAM) is an essential need for all IT organizations, not just because of the cost of software but also because of the potential litigation of copyright violation for the use of unlicensed software. Most of the organizations deploy tools for software asset management but fail to achieve the desired goals because tools are a small part of the holistic solution. This book explains the underlying complexity of SAM and includes all aspects of SAM solution that includes solution architecture, the SAM processes, tools, and function and provide a guideline to develop, build and operate an optimal solution.

Service Integration: A Practical Guide to Multivendor Service Management

Authored by Prafull Verma, and Kalyan Kumar

List Price: $15.95
5.5" x 8.5" (13.97 x 21.59 cm)
Black & White on White paper
148 pages
Service Integration
ISBN-13: 978-0692219959
(Custom Universal)
ISBN-10: 0692219951
BISAC: Computers / Information Technology

This book is intended to present a simplified guide for IT generalists who are new to the service integration subject. The purpose of this book is to educate all IT professionals with the basic concepts of service integration. Additionally, the purpose is to provide the core guidance and foundation guidance to Service Management professionals, upon which they can build and implement the service integration in their environment.

Foundation of IT Operations Management: Event Monitoring and Controls

Authored by Mr. Prafull Verma, and Mr. Kalyan Kumar

List Price: $15.95
6" x 9" (15.24 x 22.86 cm)
Black & White on White paper
138 pages
Foundation of IT Operation
ISBN-13: 978-0692205709
(Custom Universal)
ISBN-10: 0692205705
BISAC: Computers /
Information Technology

In IT operations, event monitoring and control - where you continuously monitor the health of IT infrastructure and take proactive measures to prevent the interruptions in IT services- is dominated by tools and technology, but there is a meticulous process behind it. This book tries to demystify the underlying process for this kind of operation management. There are a lot many books on service management, but those books do not cover this subject adequately and leave this area to be addressed by tools and technology. Tools vendor, on the other hand, focuses on the tool part, leaving the process aspect to the service management professionals. This book fills in the void and connects both the process and the tools to provide a holistic view. The book takes an educative tone and is written primarily for IT generalists and not for the tool experts, although it would give a new perspective to tool experts also.

Process Excellence for IT Operations: A Practical Guide for IT Service Process Management

Authored by Mr. Prafull Verma, and Mr. Kalyan Kumar

List Price: $29.95
6" x 9" (15.24 x 22.86 cm)
Black & White on White paper
332 pages
Process Excellence for IT Operations
ISBN-13: 978-0615877525 (Custom Universal)
ISBN-10: 0615877524
BISAC: Computers / Information Technology

As the title suggests, the book is providing practical guidance on managing the processes for IT Services. There is a lot of guidance available on technology management in the IT industry, but this book is focusing on technology independent service management. The book addresses all the IT people from a process practitioner perspective; however, the fundamentals are presented in simplistic terms, and therefore it should be useful to all the IT people. It will describe the process engineering concept and how it can be applied to IT Service Management. It is not just about the industry-standard framework such as ITIL and COBIT, but about the common processes that are generally used in real-life operations. This book does not focus on any technology.